The Good, The Bad, and What Remains

Melanie Ebo

Cover art by Judah Ebo
judahebo.com

Bedford , Texas
www.BurkhartBooks.com

Dedication

To my sister who said,

"You should write a book."

Acknowledgments

I hope that this entire book is an acknowledgment of the true end and scope of my life, Jesus Christ. Just in case that is not clear, I want to acknowledge Him in all my ways. Thank you, God, for being so good.

I could not have written this book without my truly inspirational husband, Tim Ebo. I love you and pray that I never take for granted every opportunity to tell you so and prove it so. You have restored my faith in men, and I have never respected anyone more for reasons that the rest of the world may have to wait until the Day of the Lord to fully understand. You and me forever!

Erin Soria, you have made this process better with every question. Thanks for your fresh eyes, your giving and graceful attitude, and never losing confidence in me. Your friendship is priceless. Thanks for letting me share your hopes and dreams as well.

Pastor Stephen Chitty, when I heard you preach for the first time, I knew I was home. The majority of our relationship has taken place on Sunday mornings and Wednesday nights as you mentored me from the pulpit. Every rabbit trail and book suggestion have helped to shape my understanding of my God, but nothing more than the example you set in character and love as you lead us all in the Christian life. Thanks for being faithful. All the Ebos love you!

Norene Fiacco, I cannot thank you enough for the kind words and encouragement you gave as you prepared a final edit for this book. You taught me to write twenty-eight years ago, and I hope my writing honors you. You are a true teacher, and I am blessed to have learned from you.

Audra Mercy Ebo, maybe Jesus will give you this message. I miss you every day, more than I can express. Your life made an impression on me that continues to shape my perspective. I desire every day to fall more in love with Jesus so that I am ready to meet Him the way you did. Until we meet again … I love you.

Contents

Foreword

There is a saying old baseball fans my age believe is irrefutably true.

*"Good hitting always beats good pitching, and
good pitching always beats good hitting."*

If you think that statement is a contradiction, then you probably aren't a real baseball fan. True fans of the game believe there are realities that are simultaneously true, even when they flatly contradict each other. This kind of reasoning is one of the dynamics of baseball that make it the best game in America. Such logic is considered irrefutable yet inexplicable, and only lovers of the game are willing to embrace this strange arrangement.

Baseball isn't the only arena in which we find this paradox. Life is full of them. Try this one for instance: "The Ebo household is one of the most ordinary families I know, and the Ebo household is one of the most extraordinary families I know."

My experience confirms the statement is both true and contradictory—at the same time!

The Ebo tribe struggles to get by one day at a time. Sometimes they win, sometimes they lose—just like the rest of us. Their battles are our battles. Their processes and problems are just like any other normal family in America. They are an ordinary family.

I also have seen something in them that I don't always see in other families. I have been their friend and pastor for years. I have seen them live out their faith up-close and personal in some of the most difficult trials imaginable. I have walked with them through a confusion of voices and perspectives on matters of faith that sometimes seemed contradictory. Tim, Melanie and their children have walked a long journey through the Valley of the Shadow of Death, and they have emerged having been refined like pure gold. My testimony of them is that they are most extraordinary!

Not every family survives a journey like theirs. I've known precious folk, some of the saints of God, who got lost in the dark valley. Some of them opted for anger or bitterness, held hostage by unanswered questions and unresolved matters of faith.

The Ebo family, by the Grace of God, got through in one piece. When I say that, I don't mean they understood all of God's ways. I don't mean they emerged unbroken. But they were broken in the right places. Relationships remained intact, and divine purposes and prerogatives were embraced. Some theological assumptions, cliched formulas, and carnal expectations did break - but they needed to be broken. God's ways are not just a better version of our ways; they are altogether different.

I can recommend this book to you without reservation because I was privileged to travel nearby during their journey. I tried to walk in intimacy without intrusion. I saw them travel with faith, trust and humility, and amazing determination. I saw this in parent and child alike. I saw it in Audra. Whether they were in high moments of celebration or in the pit of inexpressible grief, they kept embracing Jesus, and they did it over and over again.

No family should have to go through what they went through. The death of a child isn't fair, and I can't make it look or feel better with platitudes and one-liners. But I believe that everyone who shared Audra's life and passing will never be the same. Because of Audra, heaven is more real to me. Because of the Ebo's faith and spiritual response, Paul's words have taken on eternal consequence in our family:

For I am convinced that neither death, nor life,
nor angels, nor principalities, nor things present,
nor things to come, nor powers, nor height, nor
depth, nor any other created thing, will be able
to separate us from the love of God, which is in
Christ Jesus our Lord.
Romans 8:38,39 NASB

Thank you, Melanie, for telling us about the walk the Ebo family took through the Dark Valley. It is a story we will treasure forever. We love you!

Stephen Chitty, Sr. Pastor
Christian Life Church, Columbia, South Carolina

Introduction

I have a standing joke that my life is like a bad country song, without the cheating and the beer. Most of the time I don't even like to get into the details because I expect the person I'm talking to, to think, "OK, she's just making this up." I am telling you like a friend, you can't make this stuff up! Although the difficulties I have faced may not be every man's experience, I'm sure there are others throughout the world who have faced much worse. I am not looking for anyone to feel sorry for me or even sing along. When sharing my life with others, I'd like for an impression of God's goodness to remain. In fact, despite a consistent onslaught of negative circumstances, I am increasingly convinced that God is good. And I trust the Lord.

I came to this conclusion, not on my own, but through God's Word, His people, and my pleasantly unpredictable, daily walk with Him. He never promised smooth sailing in this life. One barely starts reading in Genesis before being confronted with stories of pain, difficulty, suffering, negative consequences, fear, and what appears to be injustice. But before it all sinks in with the questions, "Really? What is going on here?" God shows up to reveal a plan and His power to carry out that plan, power that cannot be withstood.

One of my favorite examples of the good plan of God is in the life of David. David was anointed king of Israel before he had any kind of formal training. He was chosen at a time when no one else—even the priest who anointed him—thought he was a good choice. He was the youngest in his family, overlooked and sent off to care for the sheep while the rest of the family handled the important things. But God had other plans for David. And that's all that really mattered. David's ascent to the throne was not immediate or easy. God had a special, post-anointing training program in mind for him. With each set-back, difficulty, or life-threatening experience, David became more grounded in the Lord and more prepared for the throne.

At one point in David's journey his band of brothers, his mighty men that always had his back, turned on him. While David and his men were off warring in another country, the Amalekites attacked David's city and ran off with the wives, children, and all the possessions of David and his men. Nothing was left. The men were so grieved that they blamed David and even talked about stoning him. David had been walking the earth long enough to have written a few country songs of his own. But because he had been walking with the Lord, his refrain was less lament and more like, "I will bless the Lord who guides me; I will not be shaken, for He is right beside me" (from Psalm 16). He knew, not just in theory, but in practice, that God is Good! David consistently included God in his life and pointed others toward Him. So, the story goes, he strengthened himself in the Lord his God. He then once again, inquired of the Lord.

A holy habit developed in David's life. He would get bad news; he would inquire of the Lord. He would see the enemy approaching, and David would inquire of the Lord. His people would tell him of some injustice or impending danger, and David would inquire of the Lord. Every time, without fail, the Lord would answer David with a good plan and the power to carry it out. As a result, that day David and most of his men (some chose not to go) followed the leading of God and went to rescue that which was taken. They overtook and struck down the Amalekites from twilight until the evening of the next day and recovered everything. The Bible says, "Nothing was missing, whether small or great ..." (1 Samuel 30:19 ESV).

I want to be described as a person after God's own heart, like David. And I think it all begins with taking my uncertainty and my need to God. I have lived through sorrow, pain, confusion, unfulfilled desire, and defeat. And my life has become much more than survival by forgetting what I think I know and depending on God, by acknowledging Him and allowing Him to direct me. By embracing each season as an opportunity to inquire of the Lord. I am not claiming that I have been perfectly obedient or even promptly obedient. But I have taken step after step, advancing with God through marital strife, letting go of dreams, picking up new assignments from God, living as a sojourner and bond-servant, pressing through spiritual struggle and persecution from those I love most, and enduring the profound stress that accompanies cancer.

Hebrews 12:27 talks about a shaking that occurs so that everything that cannot be shaken may remain. A shaken life is not pleasant during the disruption. But the promise is that what cannot be shaken will remain. The shaking is really a beneficial plan of God. From start to finish of each difficulty, challenge, trial, inconvenience, and duration of suffering, that which entangles and hinders us from making progress falls off. What is left, crosses over with us to eternity. When we are finally translated into a never-ending experience with God, the shaking will have fashioned us into kings and queens, reigning with Him. Ruling with God throughout eternity, fulfilling His eternal purpose, takes some preparation. At least as much preparation as it would take to rule with God on the earth.

God is not a formula or a principle to be practiced until we get it right. He is a perfect, living being that wants a real relationship with you and me. I am still not over that. I hope God uses this book to expose the lies of the enemy that keep you silent and alone. At the same time, I hope it encourages you to become bare before your Creator, the one with the plan and power for you. I hope it inspires you to pursue Him.

Pursuing God has never made my life circumstances magically come together, but it has most definitely been the journey that has shaped me better than I could have shaped myself. It has allowed me to move forward and remain stable and fixed in my faith through places of suffering and responsibility—to continue walking with Him and making spiritual progress, maybe not leaps and bounds, but definite progress.

I want God to be glorified and you, the reader, to be blessed by this book. Please, Father, do what only You can. Empower this book to carry out Your plan.

Chapter One

Fine, I'll Suffer

I can't remember exactly why I chose to go to chapel. I was enrolled in a small, Christian college just outside of Boston, and I confess I skipped more chapel services than I attended. It was easier my senior year because I was married and lived on the outskirts of campus; which allowed me to stay distanced from most of college life. But that day, I got up early, got ready, and went to chapel. Brennan Manning happened to be a visiting speaker, and he told the most beautiful story of a man who developed a relationship with Jesus by sitting in a room with an empty chair and inviting Jesus to sit in it. When that man became seriously ill, his family moved the chair next to his bed. He passed away with his head on the chair—resting in the lap of Jesus. The image of love and peace, even in death, made me hunger and thirst for the same. I went home that day, sat in my living room, and had a talk with Jesus.

"They said if I imagined You in a chair sitting across from me, and talked to You, that You would answer me! Well, here I am. Talk!" I demanded. "I don't know what You want from me. My life hurts to live it, and I feel like my heart could explode. I thought I was following Your plan."

And then God interrupted my monologue. He interjected with a voice that can only be heard in one's spirit, "Melanie, I love you." It was painful and comforting at the same time. My fears and demands were carried away by a flood of tears. I became vulnerable, something I usually resented and made every effort to avoid. But this time was different. His strength surrounded me and made me safe as I placed my weakness in front of Jesus. Then He spoke again, "And I want you to love Tim."

That is where the needle ripped across the vinyl and the "warm fuzzies" came to a screeching halt. "Well, if that's what You want, You're going to have to show me how, because obviously I suck at it!" We had only been married about six months. The honeymoon was undeniably over, and I had doubts that it ever really started. I was miserable in marriage, young and quickly becoming less naive, and living in defeat. I instinctively turned to the Love Chapter in 1 Corinthians 13 (NKJV) and read the words, "Love suffers long ..." I didn't get any further. I knew what God was asking. Someone had to bend. Someone had to choose to be Jesus. We were stuck, and our lifetime of love was rapidly becoming fifteen minutes of infamy (just ask our neighbors).

God picked me. The peace and tranquility I felt reveling in His love was being overcome by a selfish drive for justice. It wasn't fair. Why me? God remained silent as I worked through my anger, but I knew He was waiting for my answer. He got to the root of what was making me miserable and stunting my growth. And I responded, angrily, "Fine, I'll suffer!"

Not the most saintly of prayers, or maybe it was because it worked. For months, I laid down my entitlements at Jesus' feet, trusting Him to care for me as I cared for Tim. God showed me how to serve Tim the way Jesus served me. For a while I obeyed the Lord through gritted teeth, running into my room declaring before God, "OK, I'll be loving and kind to him, but I want it to go on record in heaven, for all eternity, that I am doing this for You, God, not Tim because he deserves nothing!" I spent day after day suffering as I grew in capacity to show unconditional love with no response from the recipient of that love.

I know it sounds ridiculous shedding light on my months of suffering, but those months carried so much weight. They were pivotal to my developing a lifestyle that would bring benefits to every relationship I would ever have. My life felt desperate at the time. There seemed to be nothing of greater importance than getting my needs satisfied. However, my husband held a totally different perspective. My needs were quite unimportant to him while in the pursuit of getting his own met. What he needed made it impossible to give me what I needed because we had needs that were diametrically opposed. That sad fact created an environment where we then lived in direct opposition to one another.

Tim used to find things that annoyed and burdened me and made sure they were accomplished. For example, we had a small kitchen sink that was divided into two compartments. He would stack the dirty dishes he used on the center divider in a way that would cause them to tip over and come crashing down when I tried to clean them. He would lay his gum wrappers on the counter instead of throwing them in the trash can which was positioned next to the counter. He felt compelled to leave his socks on the floor next to the hamper to make a point.

His disapproval and angst toward me showed up in an abundance of little ways and some bigger ways. What made me feel loved was eye contact, lots of time together and affection. Tim was working through the baggage he brought into our marriage at the time, and he would never look me in the eye. He worked three jobs just to stay away from any conflict at home. He needed to live in a peaceful environment. I needed to resolve our differences through lengthy conversation and a plan. I did not understand the need for quiet. He also needed time to sort out the pain of his past, which meant no affection for me. He believed himself to be under no obligation to see things from my perspective, and I saw him as the only avenue through which I could secure my basic requirements for life. This was not the way I imagined love and marriage.

I can't remember exactly when I became aware that men were hounds and wanted sex all the time, but I remember believing it was the absolute truth. So, when my husband began rejecting me on a regular basis, well, I have never had a problem with turning a phrase before, but that feeling is almost impossible to accurately describe. I went into all kinds of internal chaos. I recall thinking, "I saved myself for you, and this is what I get?" I was angry, confused, lonely, and felt there was something seriously wrong with me. Everyone else I knew had to fight off their young, new husbands. I was having to fight my husband to pay attention to me. I felt ugly and ashamed. And in my natural reaction, I began talking about it to Tim until he refused to talk to me about anything. Self-righteousness set in. I started to get so angry because I had nowhere to turn, and he seemed to be living just fine with our platonic conditions.

Tim's habit to retreat into himself continued to compound my loneliness and isolation. The only way I knew how to resolve things was to push harder for my rights and my needs. That only drove him further away. It drove him so far, he stopped being involved in anything that involved me. He didn't go to church. He ate at different times than me. He hung out with everyone but me. He started coming home after I went to bed.

The only shared interest he did not back away from was our precious Cocker Spaniel, Frabs. The odd thing was Tim, the dog, and I were in some kind of a love triangle. I wanted Tim, Tim wanted the dog, and the dog wanted me. One day that became obvious when Tim went to pet Frabs, and Frabs got up and walked over to me. Tim got so angry, he swore at the dog and got up to walk away. It was the perfect illustration of the emotional trauma I had been experiencing for almost a year. I simply said, "Rejection sucks, doesn't it?"

To sum up, before I involved God in this situation, it looked a little like this: I wanted affection. I asked. No response. I played hard to get. No response. I manipulated. No dice. I cried and went crazy. He got mad, told me I was insane, and instructed me to get help. A light went on, and that's exactly what I did.

I can confirm that I went to God first. But I also enlisted the help of a wonderful counselor who made an enormous impact on my life. She taught me how to communicate directly with Tim and how to accept what he was able and unable to give me. These skills, when properly used, moved me closer to my desired end. I grew to understand Tim's difficulties as being his, not a reflection of me or even indicative of his love for me or his desire for me. In short, it wasn't about me, except that I had the ideal opportunity to be a channel for the amazing, unconditional love of Jesus Christ. That love always requires laying aside yourself and being willing to put someone else first—for me, being willing to suffer rejection and loneliness. True love, eternal love, the love of Jesus suffers long.

I could not comprehend it at the time, but I was uncovering the beauty of covenant. The more I laid my life down because of the vow I made to God and for God's sake, the stronger my bond to God became. I learned to trust Him. I did not execute God's will perfectly, but I relaxed my grip on securing what I felt I needed from Tim and suffered in relative silence (or at least complained less), when my needs were unmet. Lamentations 3:24-26 (NKJV) says, "'The Lord is my portion,' says my soul, 'therefore I will hope in him.' The Lord is good to those who wait for him, to the soul who seeks him. It is good that one should wait *quietly* for the salvation of the Lord" (emphasis added). The key here is I had to get quiet enough, long enough, to allow God an opportunity to be heard. My abundance of words and demands fashioned a deafness in Tim that could only be cured by silence and a divine, gentle whisper. The Holy Spirit can accomplish way more in one phrase than I can in a sea of explanation.

My focus turned to God and what He was asking, His plan and His power, which allowed God time and space to work in Tim's life. I stopped trying to convince and convict Tim of his sins against me, and started letting God be God, most of the time. I prayed often for what I wanted for my marriage, but I cannot stress enough that God's way and God's timing brought about a relationship between Tim and me that I could not have imagined or even known how to ask for. There is no perfect marriage, but there is a perfect God who can take any surrendered relationship and transform it into the image of Christ.

During this time, I was not living in a prayer closet with God. I was walking with Him while I came to terms with my own sinful nature, discovered the dignity for which I was created in Christ, and worked to graduate from college. This is the first time I learned to suffer and not faint. I had to keep fulfilling my responsibilities while I waited on God to change my circumstances. And there was no guarantee He was going to make those changes. I learned to worship Him in the middle of the difficulty, not just after it was resolved.

My whole life before marriage was wrapped up in me, so imagine the rude awakening I experienced when it became evident that I was not perfect. I have often said, "Marriage is not hard because of what you learn about your spouse. It's hard because of what you learn about yourself."

Through a small accountability group, I started to identify the sin that gripped my life. I was saved. I had come to salvation through the sacrifice of Christ when I was a child, but letting God be in charge of my life was unexplored territory. This group taught me not only to identify sin action but the motivation behind the sin. A pattern began to surface, and I soon had the plan and the power to sense temptation and nip sin in the bud with confession and petition. In other words, I could go to God for help before I chose to behave badly. I could go to God for my needs instead of demanding from Tim what he could not give and was never meant to give. If I did not have to act like the devil, but could choose to be like Jesus, then my marriage was truly just the beginning for Jesus and me.

At first, it was discouraging to realize that this would be a life-long process that had to be revisited daily. In time, with practice, it yielded what I was truly longing for—intimacy between my Creator and me. This intimacy held potential for growth and was unlikely to fade. I am so thankful that God graciously suffers long with me.

I've heard Tim describe the day the change began in him. He had been watching me bend and behave considerately toward him for months. One day he was getting ready to build his Jenga tower of dishes at the kitchen sink and decided not only to place them carefully in the sink but to wash them, as well. He started coming home more, moving closer to me, and going to church with me. The yelling stopped, real conversation began, and the laughter we shared when we were dating returned.

The night of our first anniversary we got into a stupid argument. I can't even remember what it was about. I left the bedroom and went to sleep on the couch, just to get some distance. The evidence of healing in our relationship occurred within minutes of my exit. He came to me, picked me up, carried me back to the bed, and put me down declaring, "You sleep here." Not a great movie ending, but a true connection was made. I finally knew I belonged with him. He wanted me there.

The unique love of God is the love that moves away from self and says, "You first. I can wait." Sometimes it feels like we are waiting forever. But usually that is because we have forgotten that those who we love unconditionally are not our source for unconditional love. Choosing to suffer in obedience to God did not end with the season of inquiring in my first year of marriage. It was just the beginning. It is an ever-growing attitude that continues to encompass every relationship in my life. I have not always had the same success with other people that God brought between Tim and me. I haven't always been open to suffering in every case. I wish I would have been. However, I have never been disappointed in Jesus and His faithfulness through every opportunity He's given me to serve—no matter the relational outcome. I pray He continues to invite me to go deeper in love with Him and toward others, so that I not only please Him, but become someone who bridges gaps between people and their Creator.

PS: I am writing this shortly after our twenty-third wedding anniversary. Over the last twenty-two years our relationship has weathered many storms and become more than what I thought I wanted. It does not look like the movies. It wasn't meant to last ninety minutes. It looks like two people who live well together and work to share the love of Jesus with each other. The proof of our healing is in the eight children God has given us. Our marriage did not turn into an affection fest. We never sit around staring into each other's eyes. But our quality time is some I wouldn't trade for anything. We know each other, and we have adapted to one another in respect and love because God, His plan, and His power are always welcome.

Chapter Two

God, Grant Me Serenity

My heart started pounding as she asked the question, "Does anything on this list stand out to you?" The list was long and varied. It laid out examples of addictive behaviors that are formed to salve emotional and mental pain. There were a few I could identify with, but one stood out as if it were printed in flashing neon. I looked around the room, surveyed the group, and wondered if I really wanted to be honest. I knew I needed help. My husband told me to get help. And the opportunity for help was brooding over the chaos of my life like the Holy Spirit over the waters at creation. I took a baby step and spoke up, "I'm afraid to tell you." Gail, my loving, "spiritual mom," was not intimidated by my reservations. She invited me to participate in a Twelve Step Bible study, and I showed up; therefore, she held me accountable to the process. "What are you afraid of?" Gail responded, "That we won't love you?" "No," I continued, "that you'll tell me I can't eat. And all I can think of is, how am I going cope without the foods that comfort me?"

I was new to the process, so Gail assured me that we had not reached that step yet. In fact, she told me to eat whatever I needed because I was only on step one. In true over-eating fashion, I was trying to swallow recovery whole. But, I learned to take things one step at a time, one day at a time. I learned to trust not only the process, but that there were others who would love me through it. That was not the last moment of fear and trembling that I experienced in this small group, but it was the one that gave me confidence to push through each subsequent fear.

My survey of the room turned up faces of compassion, not judgment. Faces that broke down my defenses. I shared my deepest, darkest regrets with these five other human beings, and they embraced me as I was. It was an unforgettable season of acceptance and safety—Christ's unconditional love in action. How could anyone be the same after that?

The Twelve Step Recovery Program of Alcoholics Anonymous was created by a man named Bill Wilson. He based his steps on an accountability plan belonging to the Oxford Group, originally called A First Century Christian Fellowship. It was an evangelistic movement in the early 1900s founded by a Lutheran minister, Dr. Frank Buchman, who promoted principles of surrender, restitution and sharing (*Serenity: A Companion for Twelve Step Recovery*, pages 15-16). Only something so rooted and grounded in Christ could bring about permanent change, especially with people who have spent a lifetime practicing coping behaviors.

Addiction, simply put, is a habit that serves my emotional and mental needs until I am so dependent that I become a servant to my habit. God never intended for us to serve anyone or anything other than Him. That's why Jesus died, to set us free. "Lord, you establish peace for us; all that we have accomplished you have done for us. Lord our God, other lords besides you have ruled over us, but your name alone do we honor. They are now dead, they live no more; their spirits do not rise … you wiped out all memory of them" (Isaiah 26:12-14 NIV). The plan of the Twelve Steps is to restore our contact with the God Who created us and to live by His power. To serve Him as Lord, not the behaviors we have embraced that give us a quick fix for the moment's demands.

This group became my place to rest in the love of God. I couldn't relax at home because, during this time my home was a battleground. With my husband, the love of God was something I was required to give, but there was not much reciprocity then. These women created a respite for me where I could be myself—the good, the bad, and even the ugly. We spent nine months bearing each others' burdens and living out the love and community of Jesus. We were not anonymous. We all knew each other and participated in a ministry together. Most of us attended the same church. And we were involved in each other's journey after hours.

I remember one night I called Gail in a panic. "I ruined everything. Everything you told me to do, I did the opposite. Tim's so mad, and now it's all ruined!" After talking me down from my emotional ledge, Gail said, "Melanie, what have you done in the past to keep your emotions under control?" So much time went by in silence that she said, "Are you there?" I assured her I was still with her, and eventually replied, "I don't think I've ever controlled my emotions." Gail spent some time helping me to conclude that worship music and time singing to God could help me find solid emotional ground. The group was there for me, the body of Christ was willing. But in their flesh, they could not be where I was every time I had a need. God could, and He was. Leaning on Him, including Him in my emotional state made my life take shape, just like the first day of creation. His presence ordered my chaos with the hope of peace and calm. Even today when my heart is overwhelmed, worshipping God through song sets me high upon the Rock and restores my soul.

While attending my small group, I was also seeing a wonderful counselor on a weekly basis. At our first meeting I was defensive and not sure what to expect. I think I started by saying, "Look, if you're just going to help me figure out how everything is my mom's fault, I'm not really interested. I need help." She was so disarming and gentle in her reply, "We don't like to place blame. Let's just get to know one another." Anne spent a few weeks listening to my problems and affirming my existence. Then she opened my eyes to my fractured way of communicating.

I walked into her office for our regular session, but this time there was a white board set up. There was simply an A written all the way to the left of the board and a B written all the way to the right. She explained that it was a picture of the communication going on between Tim and me. The A represented me, and the B was Tim. She drew a line starting at the A but moving very quickly into a mess of squiggles and twists and turns that filled the entire white board and haphazardly landed at point B. Her illustration highlighted for me the futility of our current discourse. What

I intended to say to Tim was getting lost in the anger, hurt, and confusion that was spewing out of me. Tim didn't stand a chance of identifying the lasting truth through the passing emotion.

Then she set a goal for me. She erased the mess and drew a straight line from A to B. She said, "We're going to work on being direct with Tim. Cut out all the extra, and get to the point."

I honestly never knew there was a problem with the way I relayed my feelings and desires. But because I never controlled my emotions in the past, expressing myself left the listener overwhelmed and confused. It basically sucked any motivation out of Tim to try to understand me.

Getting this straightened out was annoying. I had to practice conversation with Tim. He was aware of what Anne had asked me to do and reluctantly agreed. I started by saying things like, "Did you forget to pick up milk on your way home from work because you don't love me?" He would reply, "I'm sorry, I just forgot, but it has nothing to do with my love for you. I love you." See what I mean? Just an annoying burden in conversation. But, these informative words, over time, built a reserve in my emotional bank account. Eventually, I disassociated every action that Tim made with his overall love for me. I became aware that some things Tim would do had nothing to do with me, which instilled in me peace of mind. There was now room in my perception for mistakes on Tim's part, so that I did not have to live emotionally bankrupted. Then when we spoke to each other, it was more about what we were going to do to solve the problem of no milk and less about my own insecurities misinterpreting the facts and questioning Tim's character.

In this way, I unlocked the door to real relationship. I discovered that Tim was more often motivated by love for me than I originally thought, because I gained understanding of which actions were truly connected to love. I grew in personal strength and stability. I was no longer tethered emotionally to every choice he made, so my world was not tossed to-and-fro every time there was a lack of milk in the house. I was set free to be honest and effective instead of subtle and manipulative.

Meanwhile, back at the Twelve Step ranch, steps four and five required even more honesty and openness. With the help of the Holy Spirit, we each took a searching and fearless moral inventory of our lives up to that point. And we wrote it down. Seeing my sin on paper had a profound effect on me. It was a tangible way of acknowledging my need for a Savior. And I watched with my eyes the slate wiped clean by His forgiveness. We reviewed our moral inventories together and linked each sin action with its motivator: pride, anger, lust, envy, gluttony, greed, sloth or fear.

"My name is Melanie, and I am powerless over food." That's how my practical walk in holiness began. I was surprised to find that overeating for me was not motivated by gluttony but rather by pride and anger. Now I can recognize my triggers, solicit the overcoming power of the Holy Spirit, and make wise decisions regarding what I put in my mouth. I don't have to try to band-aid my pain with food. I can go directly to the Comforter for true healing. I no longer eat to escape. I eat to live, and do my best to live for God's purpose, not my own preservation. Don't get me wrong. I still enjoy a good piece of cheesecake, and I love a good cup of coffee, but those things are not my source. They are no longer my strength.

The process never became easy. Ease is not part of recovery. Recovery is especially taxing as self-discipline creates discomfort and even its own form of suffering. But God is so faithful. Freedom tastes better than anything edible, and He places times of refreshing and reward all along the path. I learned to turn off my obsessing mind by working with my hands. I started cross-stitching, crocheting, and eventually learned to knit. This was refreshing for me because even when I was suffering, I could bless someone else. I learned how to be there for others, while I was hurting, to be a listening ear and a safe place for others to land. The process shifted my focus from inward to outward.

One day Gail approached me and said, "You look good. I mean you look comfortable in your own skin." That affirmation struck a chord deep within me. God was making something attractive about my life. Gail wasn't the only one noticing. Tim was getting a different view of me as well. One night we were arguing, building up to another fight, when out of nowhere (I'm sure it was a God-send) I started to laugh. Tim had taken a verbal jab at me, but it was funny. It made me laugh, and it broke the tension. Tim loves to make me laugh, so he kept going. I thought to myself, "This feels so good." I was finally strong enough to laugh at myself and enjoy good-hearted teasing from my husband. Thank God it did not stop there. I was also strong enough to start thanking Tim for the good things he was contributing to our marriage, but that I was late in recognizing. Apologies for wrong doing were more freely expressed between us. And love and affection that had dried up did not flow yet, but there was a hopeful trickle.

Ironically, to this day I find it necessary to fight for peace. It doesn't just find me every morning. I fight in prayer and by reasoning with myself. I fight against negative emotions, outside pressures, and the strife often caused by so many people living under one roof. I fight the desire to take flight, to escape. I fight the temptation to feel defeated. I fight the good fight because I have been equipped by God, a sweet counselor, and my Twelve Step small group of believers to stand my ground and fight—to throw off sin that easily entangles and hinders me. I know peace is possible, and I crave it. I crave peaceful living with God's Spirit and peaceful living with those around me. So, I pursue it with God's help and the tools I have obtained. Thank you, Anne. Thank you, Gail. Thank you, my forever brave friends who embarked on recovery with me. You know who you are.

Merriam-Webster defines serenity as "the quality or state of calm; peaceful." Reinhold Niebuhr wrote a prayer of serenity that has been adopted by Twelve Step recovery groups everywhere. I have prayed and continue to pray this prayer:

"God grant me the serenity to accept the things I cannot change; courage to change the things I can; and wisdom to know the difference. Living one day at a time; accepting hardships as the pathway to peace; taking, as He did, this sinful world as it is, not as I would have it; trusting that He will make all things right if I surrender to His Will; that I may be reasonably happy in this life and supremely happy with Him forever in the next. Amen."

Christ continues to answer my prayers by growing my heart's capacity for serenity, one day at a time. I trust that He will be faithful to complete His work of peace in me.

Chapter Three

Make Me Willing

The screaming would not stop. I think it had been at least forty-five minutes of blood curdling screams. I begged him to stop, but his little mind could not make the transition to peace no matter how much I insisted. Tim had left for work, and that always threw our then two-year-old son into a panic. My nerves were shot and quickly digressing into rage. My voice escalated, not just in volume but in stress level until I screamed, "Shut up, shut up, just shut up!" That's when I heard the knock on the door. I opened it to find our pastor on the other side. He said, "Everything OK? Should I come back later?" In defeat I responded, "No, come in. If you come back later, it'll be the same then."

The early days of parenthood were so hard. If I was surprised by the fact that I had to die to myself for my husband's benefit, I was blindsided by the blow of what it took to lay down my life for my kids. But that was a primary way in which God moved me deeper into relationship with Him. Tim had served as a youth pastor for a year or so before our first child came along. He was excited to be a father. I think I was excited to start a family, too, but I was probably more anxious about all the changes that would have to occur in me before I could feel confident being a mom.

After our first child was born, I did not cope very well. I was young and selfish with my time and energy. I wanted to have fun, and babies really cramped my style. I would stand over our newborn son's crib, looking at this beautiful, perfect baby, and cry through the shame of feeling stuck. I decided to share with just about everyone around me how I was done having children. One was enough for me. The faster I got this one raised, the faster I could get back to what I wanted to do. Mid-conversation with a woman from my church, God interrupted with the words He wrote all over my spirit, "You've been telling a whole lot of people what you are and aren't going to do. I think you should let Me determine how many kids you have."

I am pretty sure my response was something like, "I'm sorry, what?" After digesting it for a while, I came to the conclusion that it didn't really matter what God appeared to be asking. My husband, who told me never to ask him for more than one child, would never go for it. I could talk to Tim about what I thought God wanted, and then he would be able to say no. I would just be keeping peace in my marriage.

Tim was away at a youth retreat, so when he returned I slowly moved the conversation with him to the subject of what God had been suggesting to me. When I said, "I think God wants us to let Him determine how many kids we have," the man who I knew would not let me down, replied without a pause, "That sounds great! I think we should have a whole bus full!" What? I was exceptionally aggravated. God was not supposed to get to Tim before I did! I was so mad at God, as ridiculous as it sounds, that I gave Him the silent treatment for about three weeks.

God did get to Tim first. In fact, for a while God had been moving on Tim's heart to seek God for the next step in His plan. We had a great friend and partner in ministry at that time who spent an evening in prayer with Tim. The two of them wrestled with the idea of complete surrender and how that would practically play out. By the end of the evening, they prayed together that God would give each of them the courage to follow Him anywhere and surrender completely no matter what that looked like. God had dropped into Tim's heart the idea of His control over every aspect of our existence. The number of children we would have just seemed to slide right in to where God was leading.

An altar call at church on a Sunday night facilitated a truce between God and me. I'm not sure what the message was or why the pastor asked people to come forward, but I knew something had to give. Moving to the altar was such a great physical act of what my spirit was doing. "Lord, you can't possibly have this in mind for me. I am home with this baby all the time, and quite frankly, I feel like You are wasting so much potential." I'm not sure I ever had much humility, but God was teaching me the triumph humility can bring even if it had to start with humiliation. Once again, I sensed the Holy Spirit communicating with my spirit, "Melanie, I love you, and I want you to love Tim." At first I thought, "Well, I'm not perfect at it, but I have definitely grown in the process." And God continued, "Loving Tim means loving his children and moving forward with Tim as he moves in obedience to Me."

I wanted to cry out, "You have no idea what you're asking!" I did not want my life to revolve around one person and his needs. How lame is that? I wanted a grand purpose. I wanted to do great things for God. During that conversation, God had uncovered another layer of selfishness that made it difficult for me to make progress toward God's eternal end. Love not only suffers long, but it is not self-seeking. I had such big dreams. I wanted to be famous. I wanted to prove my worth. I still wanted a little of God's glory for myself. I imagine that's how Cain felt when he offered God what he thought was best, and God responded in disapproval. Cain tried to give something he thought was good to God. God did not want something good. He wanted Cain to be obedient to God's ways. Cain wanted to come to God on his own terms. God requires His children to come to Him on God's terms.

The scales fell from my eyes, and I saw clearly my own big-picture motivation. I could not do anything but surrender. I could not fix the problem with my stubborn heart, but God could. The Lord put a prayer in my heart that I prayed for years and still revisit at times. "I will not merely walk but run the way of your commandments when you give me a heart that is willing" (Psalm 119:32 AMPC). Please Lord, give me a willing heart.

That prayer carried me through so many acts of obedience. And it provided a repentant heart when I chose disobedience. I wrestled every single time I got pregnant. After my second child was born, I wasn't sure I would ever sleep again. I was awake for three days. I called my mom and begged her to come help. My first son was only fourteen months old, and I was exhausted. My poor

mom was so upset, but she could not get off work, and we lived
states apart. She said to me, "Melanie, you had these children
because you felt that's what God wanted from you, and this is
what it's like." I replied, "Am I being punished for my obedience?"
Mom said, "No, of course not. But you're just going to have to
rely on God for the strength to get through this."

I was in shambles emotionally and physically at my limit. I
went to the bathroom to escape all the people that needed me
all the time, and God gently spoke to my fainting heart, "If you
feel like you can't trust Me with this, it's OK. Do whatever you
need to do." There was no condemnation, just compassion for my
suffering. And then a light went on.

"What? If I feel like I can't trust You? Where does that leave
us, then? I don't want to go backwards or stand still. I want to
move forward with You." I knew what that meant. I had to learn
to trust that every time He created a new life in me, it would
mean that God was creating new life and strength and peace for
me, as well. I very much wish I was a faster learner. That would
have been helpful in my daily routine. But the majority of the
time I barely got off the couch, the house was a mess, laundry
everywhere. The kids were mostly clean, but I was not always
personally clean. And then, Tim would come home every couple
of years or sooner and say, "Hey I think we're supposed to move to
(fill in the blank here)." I was having a baby just about every year
and moving almost every two years. Life seemed so messed up.

I was angry that Tim appeared to have it relatively easy.
He got up, went to work, spent time ministering to others and
being a part of everything I loved to do. Then he would come
home for ten or fifteen minutes, get all the love and attention he
wanted from us and move right back out into a world of grown-
up conversation and rewarding work. I was home through all
the dirty diapers, spitting up, crying, screaming, and isolation.
He never complained about the absolute wreck the house was
in, or what a wreck I was, either. Even so, I was angry, and I
felt abandoned.

One day both boys started screaming for no apparent reason, and nothing I did could fix it. I called Tim on his cell phone and let them scream into his ear for about thirty seconds. Then I added, "In case you were wondering, this is what I'm dealing with today!" To top it all off, I immediately hung up. I don't know what I hoped to accomplish. I desperately wanted someone to change my circumstances. I wanted someone to make this act of obedience easier. I wanted surrender to mean an immediate rescue from the tough stuff, to mean relief from suffering.

Thank God, He meets us where we are. He even met me on my couch. During the boys' nap, I was surfing the channels and landed on a locally known speaker at that time, Joyce Meyer. Her message went something like this, "Some of you are praying for a world-wide ministry, and you can't even get victory over a sink full of dirty dishes." It was like she was looking through the TV into my disarray, and not just the state my house was in. God spoke up and assured me that He was pleased that I had chosen to be obedient. However, He made it very clear that now it was time to be obedient with joy.

Becoming a parent does something for your understanding of obedience. It's not always good enough to just do the act, although as parents we will take right behavior from our kids. However, attitude makes a huge difference in whether or not we feel obeyed. God loves a cheerful giver. Giver of what? Whatever we offer to Him—even our obedience.

There was no way I could have understood why God seemed to be so hard on me at the time. But God's perspective held what would be waiting for me down the road if I did not promptly come to grips with this part of my life. My struggle with obedience in motherhood was creating a problem between my oldest son and me. I was angry most of the time. With my whole heart I wanted to reject what God was asking of me, and my son, who was only a toddler, interpreted that anger as a rejection of him. Being obedient is vitally important, but the manner with which we obey is equally important because of how it affects those around us. I am grateful

God intervened before I created long-term damage between my oldest and myself. The truth was I loved him completely. I couldn't imagine my life without him. I also could not stop obsessing over the fact that his life required so much of mine. And that he was only the first of what would potentially be many.

Initially this act of obedience required more from me. However, with each new mouth to feed the stresses and pressures began to increase for Tim, also. As our family increased in number and the children grew, surrendering control to God constructed a paradigm for both of us that kept us moving along a well-lit, albeit narrow and even, at times, harrowing path.

What can change a negative attitude? A willing heart. I wanted to run the way of God's commandments, but I was stopped in my tracks by how the will of God conflicted with my own. Please Lord, make me willing. I wish I could give you one example from my life where I prayed, God answered, and life changed instantly or even I changed instantly. I don't have one example of that. I guess that is why God gives us a lifetime to prepare us for eternity with Him. What I can offer is that every time I have come to God with my need, my shortcomings, my desire to be willing, He has never left me on my own. He walks with me step by step through His plan and provides continual power to carry it out. Because of Him, year after year my heart continues to grow toward my children.

From the time I stopped contending with God over motherhood until now, I have been able—sometimes eventually able, but able none-the-less—to say yes to eight children, sleeplessness, lack of privacy, nothing ever going as planned, a loud home, never enough money and yet always having our needs met, more things broken than working correctly, non-stop laundry, referee-like status, and a homeschool education for eight students. And through the struggle, I have found such an increased appreciation for the life God has chosen for me. In fact, I cannot imagine it differently. I don't want to. Who knew that this life was the true desire of my heart? God did. Nothing has intimidated me as much as motherhood. But

God has given me a willing attitude and an attitude of prayer, and that has made all the difference.

Stormie Omartian said in her book, *The Power of a Praying Parent,* "None of us are perfect, so how can we be perfect parents? It's being a praying parent that makes the difference. And that's something we all can be" (page 29). That gives me so much hope. My oldest is nineteen and getting ready to leave the house as I write this. He is a unique child of God who is making such great strides to be more like Jesus. I know from the bottom of my heart that it is only because we serve a big God with a big grace that covers him. I used to look at my kids as assignments from God. God has changed my heart through willingness, and I can honestly see them, each one, for the gifts they are. I am the blessed one to be chosen to raise them.

Blessed does not mean I am an at ease, completely self-less, perfectly performing person of Pintrest, who finds motherhood exhilarating. I find most of motherhood exhausting. I do try hard to make family moments together that we will always remember. To be honest, that is all I really have confidence that we can make—a moment here and there. You try bringing ten different people together for just one evening of significance! But just because I am not thrilled by the demands of motherhood does not mean I am lacking in conviction of how precious each child is.

I want to encourage you that no matter what God is asking of you: to be a small group leader, missionary, business owner, educator, doctor or nurse, spouse, parent, care-giver to an aging parent, pastor, good neighbor, double tither, farmer, mechanic, (insert your calling here), if you find yourself unwilling, don't stop there. Enlist God's help. He is the only One Who can change an unwilling heart. He is also the only One Who can best reward a willing and obedient one.

Chapter Four

Jesus, Satisfy

"OK, Lord, here I am. I am alone in this room, the seventh living room I've had in ten years, here's Your chair. Please come and sit with me." What I wanted was a spiritual, mountain-top breakthrough and all the good feels that go with an immediate rescue. I wanted Jesus to show up and instantly fix all the troubles that were piling up around me—troubles that resulted from an honest attempt to obey God. God was leading us deeper into His will for our family and out of pastoral ministry.

A few years prior to this time, I got a phone call from Tim while he was away at a pastor and spouse's retreat. I could not attend because both boys started running a fever the day we were supposed to leave. He called to share with me his concern for our family. At this retreat he witnessed pastor after pastor giving thanks to God for bringing their children back to the Lord. Back? Why did they leave in the first place? This so disturbed Tim that he made a promise to me. "If the ministry ever gets in the way of our family, I'll leave." I thought, "That's nice," never really believing he would follow through with it.

Two years and another church later we found ourselves miserable. We had been fighting again, probably due to all the stress we were under—at church and at home. I was pregnant with our fourth and had three kids under four. If I thought Tim was absent from home at our previous church, it was nothing compared to this one. Our third child was a girl. She was not even a year old and would cry every time Tim tried to hold her because she did not know him. Our first child was three and would eat oatmeal every morning with Tim until we left ministry. Once he felt secure that he would have time with his dad, he refused to eat oatmeal again. For a year he had been choking it down because breakfast was the only time Tim was available to him. Our second son turned to screaming and banging his head on the door every time his dad left for work. Our family was visibly taking a backseat.

One day Tim was having his devotions in his office at the church, and God spoke to him very clearly, "If you lead 20,000 to Christ but lose your family, you've failed. Your family is your first ministry." That day he came home early, asked me to pray with him, and over the next few months God's direction was confirmed. Vocational ministry was over for our family.

We bowed out without a job for Tim to go to and without a specific place for us to land. From our perspective, it was a lot like when God asked Abraham to leave his home and go where God would tell him to go. We spent eight months based at my mom's house with three toddlers and a newborn. We blew through our savings in less than four months, and Tim could not find work anywhere. He was overqualified for most jobs that were accessible and lacked the experience necessary for a job that could support our family. I watched his self-respect take a slow fade with each rejected application. This could not be God's plan. It most definitely didn't look right to us, so we did not have a chance that it would look right to those around us.

We found love and support in friends and family, but we encountered little understanding. In fact, my sweet husband who is filled with integrity and loyal to a fault was confronted by a family member who believed the only reason we left pastoral ministry was because of a moral failure on Tim's part. Talk about kicking someone while he's down.

To our extended family's credit, they did everything they could to help us even though it was difficult to grasp why Tim was still out of work. We received a phone call from Tim's mom who invited us to come live with her. She had a large home that seemed empty now that his dad went to be with Jesus. She expressed her need for Tim's help to care for the house and her desire to have her grandchildren live closer. So we left my mom's and moved south. The difficulty of moving every other year ended with this move. Although I did not know it at the time, we found where

God would have us make our life-long home. However, it was another seven months before Tim landed a job. And shortly after we moved in with his mom, I found myself pregnant with our fifth.

Even while we were solvent, we experienced disapproval of our conviction to let God control our reproductive life. That was nothing compared to being pregnant without an income. Tim would say, "Just because our circumstances have changed doesn't mean God's will has changed." Man, that was tough! We never would choose to be inconsiderate of those we love, but to them, that was exactly how it came across. This was probably the only time in our lives we found it necessary to claim the scripture, "We must obey God rather than men" (Acts 5:29 NIV).

The decision to obey created copious amounts of internal, relational and circumstantial conflict. It appeared as though we were just being irresponsible and disrespectful to those who were trying to help us. Others pressed us to take a break from what we were convicted was God's desire for us. And, for obvious reasons, we were pushed away by family members who struggled with infertility. I love people, I love to please people, and I have a basic personality need for approval. I had to sacrifice all of that to pursue this call of God on my life. I do not write this easily or flippantly. I was desperate for God's vindication and for reconciliation with those around us. And so was my husband.

At the beginning of this chapter I described a meeting with Jesus. After asking Him to sit with me that day, I made a list of all the things I thought I needed to feel satisfied with my life. It looked a little like this: my own house, financial independence, friends, time to myself, understanding from our family, etc. Jesus interrupted my inventory with, "What if I told you, you don't need any of those things?" I argued, "I'm pretty sure I do! I need every one of those things." Jesus said, "None of those things will satisfy you. And, you can live satisfied and have none of those requests met." I was invited to live misunderstood, penniless, the source of others' angst, and without my own home and all that entailed. That same invitation, by the power and plan of God, was to live satisfied in Christ regardless of my circumstances.

You can't really achieve satisfaction in Christ when you link it with a list of demands, or when you are focused on outcomes that appear to be indispensable. God granted me awareness of my double-minded condition, and I laid that list at Jesus' feet that day and almost every day after that. Some days were easier than others. Every day I was reminded of what I lacked and how it was distressing to me and to those around me. But every day I was also reminded of what I possessed and the miraculous satisfaction at my disposal. I began a new habit that I would adopt for the rest of my life. My lists morphed regularly but laying them at Jesus' feet yielded the same results. Jeremiah 31:14 (AMPC) says, "My people will be satisfied with My goodness, says the Lord."

When restlessness arises, I find my way back to recognizing God's plan for my contentment. "For He satisfies the longing soul and fills the hungry soul with good" (Psalm 107:9 AMPC). He does not fill the hungry soul with stuff, thank God. He fills it with good and with the only One Who is Good. I keep a prayer journal, and I have begun to pray this prayer over my loved ones as well. "Satisfy them, Father, satisfy their necessity and desire at their personal age and situation with good, so that they may be renewed; strong, overcoming and soaring in You" (Taken from Psalm 103:5 AMPC).

This journey is far from over in me. I am not writing to you from the other side. Instead, I am writing to you as we walk together, encouraging one another. Our time living with family eventually ended, but only after we gave birth to our eighth child, paid off over $35,000 in credit card debt, managed to lose the respect of every person connected with our living situation, and after living this way for thirteen years. I want to defend myself right now. I want to convince you, the reader, that every choice we made over those thirteen years was justified. I know I can't. Mostly because I am not perfect, that is no secret. But also because some things are being kept for what the Bible calls the Day of the Lord.

"Write the vision: make it plain on tablets, so he may run who reads it. For still the vision awaits its appointed time; it hastens to the end—it will not lie. If it seems slow, wait for it; it will surely come; it will not delay" (Habakkuk 2:2-3 ESV). When we see Jesus face to face, it will all be set right—the things I did wrong and the things done wrong to me. God is not up there waiting to see how long I can hold out in my current circumstances. He is actively bringing the whole of creation to the appointed time of Christ's return. The vision of everything and everyone set right is hastening to its end.

In the meantime, how do I live with the ongoing desire for vindication? I pursue satisfaction in Jesus and hold on to my trust in His timing. Fixing our eyes on Jesus is the only thing that will free us from the grip of our desires and pull of the world. He is our way through suffering, our strength to become willing, and our key to peace and satisfaction.

In Numbers 21 (ESV), the children of Israel found themselves dissatisfied with their journey, impatient to receive the promises of God, weary from the challenges, and longing for the past—which for them was slavery! They opened their mouths and the overflow cascaded out. They complained against God and Moses, their leader. God exposed their hearts by sending serpents into their camp to bite the people, and many died. They quickly realized they had sinned, and begged Moses to pray for them to be rescued. "So Moses prayed for the people. And the Lord said to Moses, 'Make a fiery serpent and set it on a pole, and everyone who is bitten, when he sees it, shall live'" (v8). If they looked at it, they were saved.

In the same way, Jesus was lifted up (John 3:14). I encourage you, just like the Israelites, to look at Him. Look at His life, His ways, His suffering, His obedience. Fix your gaze on His power and promise. Be continually reminded by God's Word that there is a day coming when justice and mercy will visibly join forces, and we will see with our eyes the complete and eternal salvation purchased by our God. We will surely live.

Receive true satisfaction from Jesus every time you are tempted to put your trust in something else to appease you. Pursue Him. Drink the Living Water and fully quench your thirst for fleeting earthly desires. If you have been wronged or have wronged someone else (and if you're breathing you will fit in both of those categories), trust Jesus. It won't be easy. You may have to suffer, for now, being judged and misunderstood. But take heart as you look to Christ, and be assured there is a day coming when all will be made clear and every act of obedience will be rewarded.

Chapter Five

Fill Me

Music has played an integral part of my life for as long as I can remember. At first I saw it as a way to win approval and find a place socially. As I grew in the Lord, I discovered it was a gift that assisted me in drawing close to Him. I was pretty sure I was born to worship God in song. And I always felt free to worship the way I was led.

Then one Sunday during our church worship service, this changed. I felt as though something was different in me. Singing the songs was not enough anymore. And I left feeling dissatisfied. I was visibly down, so Tim asked what was wrong. I said, "Worship was so great this morning, but I can't help feeling something is missing in me." That was sort of the end of the discussion for a while, but the longing in my heart was not satisfied. "Lord, satisfy my longing in worship," became one of my every day requests. But somehow, God's response was not the same to this request as it had been to my petitions for my natural needs.

Instead of feeling satisfied, even for a short period of time, the desire and longing continued to grow. Worship services became a time of frustration, not because there was anything lacking in the service, but because there was a limitation within me. I felt as if something was trying to escape from deep inside my spirit, and it kept running into a brick wall. I decided to ask for help.

Tim and I went to visit our pastor, at the time, and shared with him that we had been reading the Word of God and seeking God's direction for our lives, specifically with regard to worship. I expressed that we had already been baptized in water, but the scripture talks about a baptism of fire, and I asked, "Is there something more we need? Are we missing something?" His response was loving and kind. He encouraged us to just keep seeking the Lord, but told us we were not lacking in any way.

For a while, I tried to let it go. But then it became that relentless itch compelling me to scratch it. While asking God for clarity in the matter, Tim remembered seeing a TV preacher invite anyone who wanted to know Jesus as their savior or be baptized in the Holy Spirit to come forward at the end of every service. Early the next Sunday morning, Tim left for Atlanta.

Luke 11:11-13 (NIV) states, "Which of you fathers, if your son asks for a fish will give him a snake instead? Or if he asks for an egg, will give him a scorpion? If you then, though you are evil, know how to give good gifts to your children, how much more will your Father in heaven give the Holy Spirit to those who ask him!" I didn't hear from Tim until about 2:00 p.m. that Sunday. When I answered the phone, I heard shouting through the other end, "I got it! Praise God, I got it!" Tim's searching had ended in the beauty of God's Spirit filling him and resting on him, and it was evidenced by his speaking in tongues. I could not wait for him to get home. He promised to lay hands on me and share the gift with me.

Four hours later, he finally arrived. I was so nervous. It was like I was meeting God for the first time, all over again. I knew enough to know that I was saved, and when I received Christ as my Savior, I also received the Holy Spirit. However, God opened my eyes to see the difference between the Holy Spirit in me, the Holy Spirit filling me, and the Holy Spirit resting on me. All I knew was that wherever the Spirit was, I wanted to be there, too. I asked the Lord to baptize me in His Spirit. Tim laid his hands on me and began to pray for me. Then he started to pray in tongues. That same something that I had felt in worship for months began to rise up in me and push its way out of my mouth.

It was joy, that I could not speak in a known language, and full of glory. It was satisfaction I did not know existed. The Holy Spirit was speaking through me. And every time He spoke, happiness came with it and, for a while, a giggle. To me, it was the purest form of being used by God. My mind did not understand what He was saying so I could not corrupt it with my imperfections. And my spirit identified it as God and therefore good. I felt like I held a precious treasure deep inside me.

The following weekend I went away with some friends. Because I grew up not understanding the value of tongues and viewing them as divisive, I decided to keep my new treasure hidden. I could not wait for the others to leave the room so I could set the Holy Spirit free to pray as He saw fit. There are a few moments in my life where I can recall pure joy, and this is one of them. I loved getting alone with God to give Him full reign over my tongue. Jesus did satisfy my longing in worship, but it could not be satisfied in the way He met my earthly desires. It had to be given the way He designed heavenly and eternal things to be passed on, by His Spirit. Praying in the Spirit has helped to make things clearer in my own spirit and has moved me closer to God.

The Holy Spirit, God's Spirit, dwells in us. God and sin cannot cohabitate. The blood of Jesus covers our sin and makes it possible for the Holy Spirit to take up residence in our hearts. When our sinful nature rises up and begins to influence our behavior, we remain forgiven or saved just as a husband and wife remain married through an offense. However every offense has its price. In marriage it takes communication, acknowledging when we are wrong and changing our manner with each other to restore intimacy and familiarity.

It is no different between us and God's Spirit. If we are reckless in our personal behavior and the way we interact with others, the Spirit will not feel at home with us and will eventually lift away. He does not abandon us or manipulatively withdraw from us. He simply moves to a place He can be comfortable, at rest, free from further grief. An example from my own life plays out something like this: I am enjoying the presence of the Holy Spirit, spending time worshipping Him, and then one of my kids interrupts by knocking on the door. I yell, "What now?" I give in to my feelings of impatience, deal less than kindly with my child, and end up causing the Holy Spirit grief. After that, my time with God changes. It doesn't become pointless, but it can feel less intimate.

My behavior reminds me that the Holy Spirit and I are not as close as both of us would like. There is still room for improvement.

God has shown me another way I have been guilty of grieving the Spirit. I would like to share it through a Bible story. After the flood Noah made a vineyard for himself and got drunk on the new wine. I heard my pastor say one time, "Why was the man of God drunk? We don't know. That's the problem with [someone else's] sin. We don't know the whole story." His son Ham entered Noah's tent and saw him drunk, passed out, and naked. Ham's reaction was to share his father's embarrassment with his brothers. But Shem and Japheth chose to take a blanket, lay it across their shoulders, and walk backward into the tent so they could cover their father and not see him naked. It's interesting to me that God was less concerned with Noah falling short and more concerned with how the witnesses responded to Noah's indiscretion.

I have been guilty of being Ham. Why? I'm not always sure. Most often it was in self-defense from an attack on my character. A few times I exposed others in their sin because it was an enticing conversation, a piece of juicy gossip that made me feel better about myself for a moment. Whatever the reason, there is no mistaking the difference in the environment before and after the Holy Spirit is grieved. Every time I have exposed someone else, He lifts away from me, and everything changes until I repent. I wish I could say I'm done with this behavior. I promise I am in cooperation with the Holy Spirit to get rid of it.

My very wise pastor also said, "There's a difference between covering someone and covering up their sin. Covering someone means we're not going to let him be shamed any further. We're going to help him maintain whatever dignity he has." This is a great way to find balance in relationships where you are aware of someone's sin. There is a time and place for accountability. We need to be careful to be Spirit led, and to be motivated for the good of the other person.

The years we spent living with family seemed to escalate strife in our lives. I know strife grieves the Holy Spirit. Somewhere in my childhood I picked up an aggressive guilt that insisted true forgiveness meant maintaining close relationship (aka no boundaries) with the person one has forgiven. Praise Jesus, I have come to realize that is not healthy. Sometimes forgiveness simply looks like what my pastor said: putting an end to the perpetuation of shame and no longer exposing a person's sin. We demonstrate this by protecting his or her dignity. Love always protects.

Genesis 13 (AMPC) tells a related story about Abraham and Lot. Basically, living together wasn't working for them anymore. They had outgrown their ability to peacefully cohabitate. Abraham said to Lot, "Let there be no strife, I beg of you, between you and me, for we are relatives." And in the name of peace they did not merely separate, but they went in opposite directions. This set me free. Sometimes boundaries that limit your involvement with someone else is the only way to keep from grieving the Holy Spirit. I think the balance to this is found in Genesis chapter 14. Lot was captured by an enemy and carried away. When Abraham learned of it, he came to Lot's rescue and returned with his nephew and all the stolen goods. It does *not* go on to say that their loving support for one another convicted them to live together again.

All relationships are made peaceful through the direction of the Holy Spirit. Seeking His guidance and remaining full of His Spirit is always the priority. 2 Corinthians 3:17 (AMPC) tells us, "Now the Lord is the Spirit, and where the Spirit of the Lord is, there is liberty, emancipation from bondage, freedom." Cooperating with the Holy Spirit seems grievous to us at the time, but there is nothing worth holding on to that might grieve the Holy Spirit and lift His presence from our lives, even for a moment. God's promise, as we pursue Him is found in Psalm 16:11 (AMPC), "You will show me the path of life; in Your presence is fullness of joy, at Your right hand there are pleasures forevermore."

I am not implying in any way that your experience with God should reflect my own. I am not drawing any lines in the sand to distinguish myself as a greater Christian than someone who lives a holiness lifestyle without tongues. I can only share my experience, and God's way of leading me. I am saying, if you are in a place that seems spiritually lacking and dissatisfying, seek the Lord until He is found. Ask Him for more of the Holy Spirit. Trust Him to fill you however He chooses. Then cooperate with Him as He gently leads you to continual filling, which is His ultimate plan and power for each Christian life.

Chapter Six

Prisoner of Hope

My attempt to be seated in the pew took the form of a giant plop. I was carrying the weight of my world on my shoulders, and the burden made it hard to do anything gracefully. Tim worked the night shift through the weekends at that time, and it was extremely difficult for him to attend Sunday morning services. I carted all the kids to church and waited for strength and energy for the next week to be spoon fed to me from the pulpit. I had forgotten that this Sunday was our annual Word Spirit Power conference. I glanced over the bulletin and had a lift in my spirit thinking of the blessing I was sure to receive. This conference was always well prayed over, and I can't remember one where God did not bother to show up and make His presence known.

RT Kendall was the first to speak. He was preaching on joy of all things. I was carried away by the depth of his message until he stopped abruptly and said, "There's someone here who is in the fight of their life. They aren't sure they're going to make it because they're operating in their own strength, and the Lord wants them to receive His joy." Something stirred in my spirit, but I thought, "I wonder who it is." He continued with his message and reiterated at the close that the Lord was strongly urging an individual to allow Him to do a work of joy in his or her life. As he took his seat, my heart started beating faster. The other two preachers that spoke after him are always amazing, but I can't even remember what they said. When God commands your attention, He holds it.

At the end of the service an altar call was given. People came forward to allow God to minister to their hearts for so many reasons. Then RT expressed once again that it was not too late, that God was speaking specifically to someone and that person should come forward to receive from God. I looked around frantically, hoping to see someone else move forward. There were no takers. People were responding consistently until Dr. Kendall would extend an invitation to the person God wanted to heal with joy. I thought my heart was going to pound out of my chest. I knew God was speaking directly to me.

I was a victim once again of situational weariness. Jesus was still carrying me through my daily responsibilities, but my mind wandered to thoughts of better days. I wanted to live in my own house, call my own shots, live independently of the aid of others, put my children first instead of the interests of others to whom I was obligated. I wanted change in my circumstances—life's circumstances that had grown stale and were becoming more demanding year after year. I found myself completely worn out and out of practice at being positive. I fell into a rut and fixed my mind on what was wrong instead of the One Who is always right.

Therefore, I let the invitation go by. Service ended, and I was still stuck in my seat. Oddly enough, RT Kendall had not yet left the platform. The Lord spoke to my heart one more time, and thank God, I decided it's now or never. I walked forward and thanked Dr. Kendall for his message and explained that I was the person God had been speaking to. I love how he dealt with me that day. He simply said, "Oh. Well let's move off the platform to the bottom of these steps."

I do not come from a Pentecostal background. So my first thought was, "No need. I am not going to pass out." He did not need to move me to a safe place, because I would not be falling down. I mean it was OK for other people, but I wasn't comfortable with it, so I would not be participating. I followed him anyway, and thank God an usher decided to help. All RT did was raise his hand toward me and say, "Joy!" Then he left and let God do the rest. I absolutely love that. I was powerless to control anything that followed because when I moved toward God in obedience, I gave Him the control. He decided it was time for me to experience the weight of His glory.

I have heard that expression before, "the weight of God's glory," but I always interpreted it as a symbolic weight. What I experienced that day was an actual, physical weight that fell on me and slowly pressed me to the floor. It sounds like a contradiction, but it was gently overpowering. It did not leave me feeling helpless and afraid of losing control, instead it created an environment where I felt truly safe. I didn't pass out. I was completely aware and completely caught up in the Spirit of God. While lying there, I started to feel peaceful, happy, and lacking nothing. It was not because the stresses of my life had changed, but because I was held there, fixed on Christ by Christ, and nothing else could interfere. I don't know how long it lasted. It lasted long enough for my strength to be renewed. And it made an impression on me of just how much God can accomplish in a few moments of uninterrupted focus. It may seem unrelated to say that joy renews strength, but Nehemiah 8:10 (NIV) reminds us at the end of the verse, "… the joy of the Lord is our strength." Sometimes merely getting stronger is not enough. We need the joy that continually renews and sustains.

Later I would understand that it wasn't just a feeling of peace and happiness that had been imparted to me, it was a seed of eternal hope. Experiencing pure joy, without any of my concerns specifically addressed or rectified, gave me deep confidence in the transcendence of my God. He took restorative action that day and revealed to me the depth of His provision—His plan and His power. My perception of my problems was reduced to an afterthought when I encountered the magnitude of the Presence of the all-powerful God. I could not escape the conclusion that everything would be alright.

Proverbs 13:12 (ESV) explains, "Hope deferred makes the heart sick, but a desire fulfilled is a tree of life." If unfulfilled hope in a specific desire can make you heartsick, imagine being stuck in circumstances so long that you start to put off hoping altogether. I've always thought Abraham must have felt that way. When we started out after we left vocational ministry, I remember thinking, "I don't want to wait twenty years for God's promise to be fulfilled, like Abraham. I want direction and security." But life with Tim unemployed meant we had to trust in the provision of God and the generosity of others without the benefit of any of the details. Sojourning twenty years like this was not an acceptable idea to us. But God was teaching us to endure.

The natural progression of our difficult living conditions put me in the position of a bond-servant. I know that when we moved in with my mom-in-law, we were already a force to be reckoned with, but our family doubled in size before we moved out. It was difficult for her. She had to flex and bend with regard to the things that were most important to her. My mother-in-law and I are polar opposites in personality. It is not hard to imagine our frustration in living together. Our ways did not line up, our daily routines did not match, and our expectations could not have been more different. We would be challenged by so much agitation in our environment, and then we would challenge each other. Every time I had to back down. She held the trump card. She owned the house.

Tim's mom had a relationship with Jesus that began in childhood. Therefore, we had the most important thing in common. And we shared the most important people in our lives. But being in such close proximity and never getting a break seemed to amplify our differences. She had complete autonomy over her house and felt no inhibitions to keep it that way. Rightfully so. However, that authority began to push its way into other aspects of my time, attention, and responsibility. If she was feeling unmotivated to handle her own personal tasks, she felt justified to put them on my shoulders. If she had a need, it was communicated as priority number one for me. My agenda was governed by her desire. And ultimately, her drive to assure her needs were met overwhelmed me in my desire to keep peace and fulfill my separate responsibilities.

None of my mom-in-law's actions or expectations were evil. And they would never have existed outside of our living under the same roof. They were simply without regard for what it cost me in my daily living. That left me with a bitter taste in my mouth that drove me to my knees. I spent so much time begging God to change my circumstances and looking for a way out that I lost sight of the change God wanted to do in me.

One day, my time in God's Word led me to the part of Abraham's story that included Hagar. In Genesis 16 (ESV), Hagar not only looked for an escape, but she made a run for it. Who could blame her? She had no choice in the circumstances which tormented her. She was a servant following the will of her mistress. But God interrupted Hagar's escape and said, "Return to your mistress and submit to her." That makes no sense. Our Great Rescuer was sending her back to a completely unfair situation, asking her to submit to a self-serving authority? That's exactly what God was asking, but He did not ask her to return empty-handed. The reward for following God's plan was that God Himself would care for Hagar's interests. She no longer needed to secure fair treatment from others because God held her world in His hands. "So she called on the name of the Lord who spoke to her, 'You are a God of seeing,' for she said, 'Truly here I have seen him who looks after me'" (Genesis 16:13 ESV). Hagar now possessed a hope for the future that would endure with her.

I'll admit my story shares few similarities with Hagar's, but one way in which I identified with her was that I wanted to escape my mistress. She did not beat me or aggressively mistreat me, and I begged God to keep me from holding her in contempt. At a time in my life where my family could have suffered immense difficulty, living with Tim's mom meant my children never missed a meal, let alone went hungry. We were warm and cared for, and in reality, we were grateful. But at the same time, we were a burden. She persisted in reminding me of my obligation to serve her needs. It was especially difficult because I did love her, but that would never change the fact that I lived indebted to her. I grew weary of obligation and longed for the day when love would be all that was necessary between us.

I did not realize it at the time, but when I took my seat at the Word Spirit Power Conference, I had already been guilty of laying aside hope for my life to ever change. God had a plan. Not to resurrect my old hope, but to plant His own enduring hope deep in my spirit. And as it grew in me it became a hedge of protection from all the circumstantial negative that would threaten my faith. It grew and grew until there was no escaping, and I could honestly say, "I am a prisoner of hope."

Zechariah 9:12 (ESV) says, "Return to your stronghold, O prisoners of hope; today I declare that I will restore to you double." I know this scripture was given directly to the children of Israel. However, Zechariah was prophesying of the coming of Christ Who came for all, so I don't believe I am misusing this verse by saying it is a promise on which we, too, can depend. The definition of the word prisoner is a person captured and kept confined. That is the perfect description of the way my encounter with God's Spirit played out. I was captured by hope in my Savior and kept confined by assurance of His goodness. That did not mean I chose only rose-colored vision and an optimism that pretended the facts did not exist. Instead it became a stronghold, a place of strength where every doubt was inspected and every fear acknowledged and then eventually placed in the capable hands of God. Most of the time I learned to take a long hard look at the difficulty in my life and then weather it with calm confidence that God would act on my behalf.

I did not go home that day and become perfected in my responses to my mistress. I learned to accept my position as bond-servant because I was assured it was only temporary. Even though it would be years until I was released, those years I lived in hope, submitted to God and to my mom-in-law. Most days I was able to keep her away from displays of my frustration, and I focused on serving her every time the devil tried to tempt me to resent her. I took inventory of the reasons I was grateful for her and took the time to say so. Our relationship did not shed its difficulty while we lived together. In fact, little changed in her expectation, but my expectation shifted. I learned to ask God to identify my responsibility every time she made a request. Eventually, I could say no to some things which made room for me to fulfill my responsibilities as wife and mother. I learned to be guided by what pleased the Lord. While it changed little in the temporary, I was enduringly hopeful it would make all the difference in the eternal.

God did move and eventually change some of my circumstances, but not all. He did answer some specific prayers the way I asked but not all of them. He continued to give me hope through a second battle with unemployment for Tim, cashing in our retirement, four miscarriages, and almost losing our newborn son. When our eighth child was born, he was three weeks early and tiny. He weighed about five pounds, and a silver dollar would have completely covered his eyes, nose and mouth. He was so precious, and two weeks after he was born, we were in the PICU (Pediatric Intensive Care Unit) asking God to spare his life.

The reality was our son was failing to thrive. Every minute brought lower body temperature, increasing blue skin color and extreme listlessness. The doctors worked to rule out anything and everything that might be wrong, which meant a lot of needles and tubes and contact precautions. I couldn't even hold him to reassure him that he was not alone. While getting settled that first night in the PICU, everything sank in, and I cried out to the Lord, "He's dying. He's not going to make it through the night. So if You want him to live, You're going to have to do something." The next morning our son experienced a miraculous turn. That journey was not over that day, but within two weeks we were home, and he was finally thriving. Those two weeks were some of the worst days of my life up to that point. I never could have prepared myself to watch my baby suffer. And being away from my husband and children was so challenging. The whole experience was taxing, revealing, and stretched me beyond my previous capacity.

Love suffers long, but what if the suffering is put on the one you love? Love protects, but what if you don't have the power to protect the one you love? The place where your ability ends and you invite God's ability to begin, that is where hope engages. Hope surrounded me with the image of God as Healer and Jesus as taking up residence right in the middle of my pain. Quiet confidence in the goodness of God kept me peaceful, stable, and mostly kind. I'm sure I could have freaked out with very little effort, but God was actively working in me, anchoring my heart and mind to His

Spirit. His grip kept me from drifting away into darkness. I was confined by the hope that God was doing what I could not do.

This experience clarified so many things about God's ever-deepening involvement in my life and my circumstances. If God was present to deliver and heal my son from the grip of death, then He could most certainly deliver me from bondage and heal my relationship with my mother-in-law. He could preserve His hope in me to serve me on the days I felt most defeated. And encourage me to treat others lovingly regardless of the way I am treated. He holds my world in His hands, and He looks after me.

The proof came at the unexpected end to my mom-in-law's earthly days. I can honestly say it was a privilege to serve her during her final hours. We had been living apart for over three years, but because of twelve years of living together, I knew just what to make her for her last meal. I knew how to meet her expectation of me and felt no hesitation in volunteering any way I could be of help. When we were alone in her room, I was moved to sing from her hymnal, and found that we were not alone after all. God's presence filled the room and bridged the gap between us, and we found ourselves praising the Lord together. Loving her flowed out from what was in me, from what the Lord planted all those years before. Obligation disintegrated, and all my prayers for right relationship were granted.

All things lie dead in the water without hope. Hope is an amazing gift. If you find yourself lingering in perpetual weariness with the way things are, resist looking for the nearest exit, and ask God for the hope that only He can provide. Let it overtake you, surround you, and hold you captive until you find yourself settled in God's safety. Until He has restored to you double, the double that removes mountains of negative situations from your life, or even better, the more eternal double that transforms the mountain of negativity living in you.

Chapter Seven

Trust and Obey

While my husband served in pastoral ministry a singular theme emerged from his preaching. It took on a variety of fun, interesting, and challenging forms, but it boiled down to "Listen, and obey." At one point, his desire to obey was put to the test. He came home and said, "I think I'm supposed to fast for forty days." My reply was, "Fast what?" He said with a little fear and trepidation, "Food." My mind was swimming with questions. Which foods? All food? When will you start? How will you survive?

My concern was not invalid. Tim never did carry any extra weight. He needed all the muscle and flesh he had. There was nothing to spare. All things considered, he moved forward with God anyway. Nearing the end of the forty days with no food, I walked into our bathroom while he was on the scale. His body was skin and bone. I quickly backed out of the bathroom, closed the door, dropped to my knees, and begged God not to take him. I can testify that Tim truly did survive by the grace of God. When asked, Tim testifies that, by the grace of God, he can be trusted to obey.

Psalm 40:6 (AMP) tells us, "Sacrifice and offering You do not desire nor have You delight in them; You have given me the capacity to hear and obey …" When we respond to the invitation to obey, He gives us the capacity. The psalmist may not have used the word grace, but God's grace is not just a covering over us. It is the power that enables us. It is the ability God has given us to obey.

Galatians 5:16 and 24 (ESV) say, "But I say walk by the Spirit, and you will not gratify the desires of the flesh. And those who belong to Christ Jesus have crucified the flesh with its passions and desires." The desires of our fallen nature often lead us in the opposite direction the Spirit is desiring to take us. That is why obedience can be difficult and unpleasant. However, the more we obey the Spirit and keep in step with Him, the more we desire obedience and the simpler it becomes. It is very much like our physical bodies. The more we eat sugar, the more we crave sugar. The more we drink water, the more our bodies crave water. Joyce Meyer said the same thing but in the opposite way, "Whatever you starve dies. When something is dead, it has no influence anymore." We can actually starve our selfish impulses, so that their influences begin to die. At the same time, we can search out the Word of God until His influence moves us to obey.

While having my personal Bible reading one day, I came across a scripture I had read many times, but the amplified version caught my attention, and became a catalyst for change. Psalm 1:1 instructs us, "Blessed, happy, fortunate, prosperous, and enviable is the man who walks and lives not in the counsel of the ungodly, following their advice, their plans and purposes, nor stands submissive and inactive in the path where sinners walk, nor *sits down to relax and rest* where the scornful and the mockers gather" (emphasis added). Those words caused my mind to flash back to scenes from some of the TV shows I was choosing to relax and rest with. It was eye-opening to me. But it did not stop there. I realized I could not even be in the house unless the TV was on. Because silence made me uncomfortable, all day long the noise of the world was pouring into my head.

Please don't misunderstand me. I am not anti-movie or anti-television. In fact, I really enjoy a good movie, and I love the BBC. Back then, I was powerless to turn it off. Whenever something holds power over you, God will expose it for what it is so that you can find freedom. Please follow His leading, and do not use my story as an opportunity to pick up a few more laws.

The plan was to starve my need for noise, specifically TV noise for forty days. What's crazy is after those forty days were up, that medium no longer had a grip on me. I found myself able to turn off a murder mystery show and go to bed before the mystery was solved. And that was back before DVRs! Entertainment finally took its proper place in my life and served its intended purpose. It was no longer my constant companion when I was alone. God gained more ground in my life. He started to fill the void.

As I attempted to walk in step with the Spirit, He shed light on other things that kept my attention divided. But each of the individual issues seemed to have one far-reaching root. I was very interested in my personal comfort and convenience, and that focus was hindering me. In Matthew 16:24 (ESV), Jesus describes the cost of being His disciple, "If anyone would come after me, let him deny himself and take up his cross and follow me." The cross is the place where comfort and convenience do an about-face. They are no longer acknowledged and accommodated in a life that follows after Christ. Picking up our cross means we let go of our desires, deny ourselves. It is a suffering that is unique to the cross. Sometimes we suffer because we live in a fallen world. Junk happens to us that we have no control over. But the cross, that is a different matter. If we are committed to following Jesus, we lay down our selfish desires and ambitions, and we pick up obedience to Him. The cross is a choice to suffer. It is a slow and painful death of all that is self-seeking within us.

It hurts to live and die by the cross. It is, however, the only lifestyle guaranteed to produce eternal reward. "... that I may know him and the power of his resurrection, and may share his sufferings, becoming like him in his death, that by any means possible I may attain the resurrection from the dead" (Philippians 3:10-11 ESV). If we lose our low-level quality of life for the sake of Jesus, He promises that we will find a regenerated life of an abundant quality (Matthew 16:25, John 10:10).

Keeping an eye on the prize is an important part of our walk with Jesus. Hebrews 12:11 (ESV) reminds us, "For the moment all discipline seems painful rather than pleasant, but later it yields the peaceful fruit of righteousness to those who have been trained by it." Discipline is another word for training, and God's training program will always involve denying yourself. One year after Tim completed his forty day fast, God included the same training for me. I was not excited. In fact, up to this point I regularly thanked God that He never asked that of me. So, when I felt prompted in my spirit to give up food for forty days, I resisted for about two months.

Finally, I could not escape God's nudging. I went forward in church to pray for strength. My pastor put his hand on my shoulder, and without even knowing my specific fears, he named and stood against each one in his prayer. Then he stopped and said, "I keep seeing this picture in my mind of you and the devil. He's got you cornered and convinced that you can't do this. But I think it's because you don't understand the power of the sword you wield." He ended our prayer time praying over me in the Spirit. Something rose up from the depths of my spirit, and I began to pray in tongues with him. When I left there, I was confident that God had all this under control. I had been given the capacity to obey.

Capacity is not another word for ease. It sometimes means we get to the end of an act of obedience and think to ourselves, "Wow. That was kind of ugly and only by the grace of God." Walking out a forty day fast while caring for the needs of a husband and six children was miraculous at least. I don't remember it being a particularly warm, fuzzy experience. I do remember the hunger pangs, the crying out to God for help, and the times I had to walk away when I was frustrated and reactive. I also remember how God did not stand in judgment, but walked beside me as my daily Portion.

This step of obedience yielded for me an irrepressible desire for God's Word. I learned to read the Bible in a way that energizes and fuels my life. Just like real food, we take in Scripture on a regular basis so that we have energy to engage and fulfill the demands of life. While denying yourself in a food-fasting situation, it is imperative to saturate yourself with God and the things of God. I learned to recognize Jesus as the Word, my daily Bread. I do not remember my first encounter with scripture, but I do remember this is when it became a part of my steady diet. At the completion of the fast, I ate the best tasting boiled tomatoes I ever had. And then I was consumed with an appetite for the Bible that led me straight through it, reading from cover to cover in nine months.

I don't think there is anything magical about the order in which you read the Word, but I felt a push in my spirit to start in Genesis and read all the way through Revelation. I bought a notebook and decided I would begin to look for descriptions of God on every page. I wrote down declarations like this:

You Are:

- God, Who prepared, formed, fashioned and created the heavens and the earth
- God Who speaks and Your words are always manifested
- God Who sees that all You have created is good, suitable, and pleasant, and You approve it completely
- The One Who separates light from darkness
- God Who put the stars in the sky as signs and tokens of Your providence
- God Who blesses His creation to be fruitful and multiply
- God Who created man in His own image and likeness
- Love, You love me, and You want me to love others like You do
- For me, not against me

And the list goes on to fill almost two notebooks with word pictures of God. I seized the opportunity to search out my God and found His character to be trustworthy.

I had a zeal for this adventure that left my husband annoyed and a little jealous. He complained that I could get blessed by the genealogies. He was just teasing me, but seriously, the moment I finished reading about all the chaos, violence, wandering and sometimes seemingly ridiculous events of the Old Testament, I poured over the generations listed in Matthew. Matthew's list completed the recording begun in 1 Chronicles 1 from Adam to Abraham and brought us all the way to the advent of Jesus. My heart overflowed with joy at the confirmation that God always finishes what He starts. No matter how long it takes, no matter how many side roads we go down, He brings us around to His purpose. Man has never been abandoned by His Creator. God has been actively working for the benefit of mankind, to bring about all He has planned, from the beginning.

Reading the Bible straight through shed light on some things that confused me in the past. I used to read Old Testament stories and think, "Sometimes it seems like God is letting people get away with heinous sins." Then I would read others where He would severely punish someone for what I judged a simple misdemeanor. I could not wrap my head around it until the Holy Spirit pointed out that God's grace covers us, especially when we are in pursuit of Him. God wants to be pursued! When our children are moving forward in life, working to apply the things we have taught them, and they fall and make mistakes—sometimes big ones—we instruct and discipline. But when they rebel, push us away, and carry on without regard for us, we respond in more drastic ways to get their attention and hopefully lead them back into a place of safety. It all came together for me. And it changed my perspective on Who God is and how deeply and patiently He loves.

I find so much inspiration for obedience in the life of Abraham. He waited over twenty years to the see the promise of God fulfilled in the birth of his son, Isaac. Then Genesis 22 (ESV) tells us that God tested Abraham. God instructed him to sacrifice the long-awaited promise, Isaac, as a burnt offering. Abraham knew his God. His trust in God had been growing exponentially through their sojourning together. The Bible says, "So Abraham rose early in the morning, saddled his donkey, and took two of his young men with him, and his son Isaac" (Genesis 22:3). They set out on a journey that took three days. I know how crazy I get waiting three days for a doctor's report or to see if we'll make enough money to pay a bill. I cannot imagine the stress and anxiety he was fighting. "When they came to the place of which God had told him, Abraham built the altar there and laid the wood in order and bound Isaac his son and laid him on the altar, on top of the wood. Then Abraham reached out his hand and took the knife to slaughter his son" (Genesis 22:9 ESV).

God protected Abraham and the promise that day. Just before the knife plunged into Isaac, God spoke up and told Abraham not to harm him. He then affirmed Abraham by saying, "… for now I know that you fear God, seeing you have not withheld your son, your only son, from me" (Genesis 22:12 ESV). I don't think it was God who needed to find out anything about Abraham. God tested Abraham to prove to Abraham that God remained worthy of his trust, and Abraham could be trusted to obey God.

There are so many threads I could have followed during my read through His Word, but God had me focus on His character. To know God is to know He loves me, not because of me, but because of Who He is. I can't alter Who God is with my behavior. I can trust Him because His goodness never changes. His mercy never runs out. His faithfulness is great. I can follow Him anywhere He leads, because His love never fails. To know God is to trust Him.

If you do not have a desire for obedience or the Word of God, ask for the desire. He grants and grows our capacity. Go armed into obedience with the truth of God's Word. Enter God's training program, His plan for life and godliness. And when it gets painful, look to Jesus, "… the founder and perfecter of our faith, who for the joy that was set before him endured the cross, despising the shame, and is seated at the right hand of the throne of God. Consider him who endured … so that you may not grow weary or fainthearted" (Hebrews 12:2-3 ESV). Keep the promised rewards of joy, peace, and rightness with God at the forefront of your mind. Let God move you from being unconditionally accepted to lovingly proved. Let God show you that you, too, can be trusted to obey.

Chapter Eight

Strength and Mercy

Audra Mercy Ebo was born March 8, 2004. Her birth should have been an indication of the way in which she would take life by storm. She was number five out of what would be eight children for our family. After giving birth to number four, I knew I needed to change the labor and delivery plan. Up until then, I had not had an epidural, but baby number four was so tough, I knew I needed help. When I received the epidural things progressed very quickly. My doctor came in the room, checked my status, and left saying, "It'll be a little longer, so I'll be back in a little while." The door did not even fully close on her when I felt something pop. I looked at Tim and said, "Please ring for the doctor because something has changed." My husband, the always calm and collected, said, "Are you sure because she was just in here?" I established that I was sure, and fortunately he was able to reach her before she left the nurses' station.

Dr. Julie slipped into the room with her sweet smile and said, "OK, let's get you in position." As soon as I moved, it was obvious the baby was coming. In fact, my doctor did not even have time to put on her gloves. She bent down and caught Audra in her apron with one quick but smooth motion. "My first gloveless delivery!" she exclaimed. That was only the beginning of firsts that Audra's life would bring to all those who lived with and around her.

She was the first baby that I could have set my clock by. Her routine was not just a routine, but to the minute you could predict her waking, feeding, and sleeping again. She was tiny and blue-eyed, which was something that looked impossible for our family, but was the result of perfect, recessive, genetic alignment. By the time she reached her first birthday, she was an important contributor to our family unity. The other kids adored her and rallied around her care.

Audra's name means strength. She was about three years old when her will became more than just a set of preferences and a few temper tantrums. In fact, I have never contended with an opponent who left me feeling more defeated than Audra from ages three to seven. I prayed for her will to be broken, because I thought she might have a real shot at breaking mine. Every morning I would have about five to ten minutes of peace, and then Audra would have an issue or I would have to say "no" to her, and the war of the worlds commenced. Stress between us was tangible. And even though I was pretty sure she would survive this, I was not sure I would.

She was difficult, but absolutely adorable. She was a little girl with a deep voice, funny and fearless and full of motivation to get as much as she could out of every day. Nothing was ever enough for Audra. I would go out of my way to give her the repeatedly expressed desire of her heart, and then she would move on to something else before the first desire was fulfilled. I had to pick between the fight when telling her no, or the exhaustion when trying to say yes. Things may have been different if she would have been an only child, but I had six other children at the time, including one infant and one toddler. Audra liked being an older sister. She loved having others to boss and control. Now that I think about it, she liked bossing her older siblings as well. She was definitely controlling, but she was also fiercely loyal. She made sure nobody else messed with her brothers and sisters.

So much strife resulted from her strong will that my husband took to calling her by her full name, Audra Mercy, in an attempt to call out some mercy to temper her strength. I increased my petition and made it my daily prayer for God to break her. Then God broke through to me. He reminded me that, "… the goodness of God leads you to repentance" (Romans 2:4 NKJV). My prayer changed to, "God help me to be good to her. Help her to see You through me. Sanctify her will, and use it for Your glory."

One summer, after Audra turned seven, my oldest went to a special boys' camp and came home with a story to tell. The speaker explained to the boys how to gauge their relationship with God and how to determine their eternal future. During family devotions

Logan relayed the illustration to all of us. Audra was visibly uneasy. She kept moving around and fidgeting, and in my gentle, quiet way I responded, "Audra knock it off. Be still. What's wrong now?" The Holy Spirit stopped me. I took another look, saw that she was afraid for the first time, and asked, "Audra do you know for sure that you'll go to heaven when you die?" She responded, "I don't know." I said, "Do you want to be sure? Because you can be sure right now and for the rest of your life." She said, "OK." The next few moments were so precious. She asked Jesus to forgive her for the things she had done wrong and to come into her heart as her Lord and Savior.

The change in her wasn't dramatic, but it was consistent. She would still press for her way, but after she crossed the line and became unloving and disrespectful, she would regret it. And eventually she would come to me on her own and ask me to forgive her. That was totally new and evidence that Jesus was working with Audra to make her more like Him. The fight in her never died, it just changed. She started fighting with some brothers and sisters more often, but now it was in defense of another brother or sister. She had a love for stuff and sometimes a drive to get more, but she got better at sharing and giving. In fact, one Sunday she gathered every dollar she had and put it in a special offering at children's church. Everything in me knew this was going to stink for her when she wanted to buy something later, but thankfully, the Lord kept me from discouraging her. I did ask if she understood what she was doing. She said, "Mommy, they're poor. I want to give them something." That wasn't the last time she gave everything when a need was presented. The most recent gift was hundreds of dollars she was saving for something she wanted, but the need was so great, she just couldn't help herself. She had a bigger desire to help someone else.

Audra was extremely physically flexible and would have made a great gymnast. She used to shimmy up the doorways of our house that led from one room to another. I have pictures of her with both legs behind her neck. And splits were usually the big finish to every creative dance number she performed at the Ebo Living Room Dance Academy. Then one Sunday on the way home from church she said, "Mommy, I couldn't jump during the worship songs today. My legs hurt." I assured her it was probably nothing. I had already been through growing pains with four kids and was confident this was nothing to be concerned about.

Over the next few months symptoms of pain and rashes and appetite loss began to come and go. At Thanksgiving she grew pale and started running a fever. It went away, and I thought it was just a freak virus. The ultimate clue that something was not right was when she sat down next to the Christmas tree and said, "I don't think I can walk up the stairs and help you with the presents this time, Mom. Can I just sit here and hand them out?" That question made me uneasy, because she was not one to surrender the things she loved doing most. But we moved forward with Christmas day anyway.

Two days after Christmas was a Saturday. Audra woke up around 5:00 a.m. She came into my room complaining of unbearable pain on her right side and started throwing up. I was a little in shock, so I called Tim at work, and we decided I should take her to the emergency room. While in triage, I was asking the nurse about appendicitis, and Audra insisted she was feeling better and wanted to go home. Her symptoms were severe but would come and go rapidly. I gave in. We went home and decided we would visit the chiropractor on Monday to deal with the pain in her legs and hips first.

After examining our daughter, the chiropractor refused to adjust her. He said he did not like how she was reacting to pressure on her side and suggested we have her seen by our pediatrician right away. We left his office and went straight to her doctor's office. They fit us in, and I was convinced she had appendicitis. The doctor knew something different. We went immediately for bloodwork and an ultrasound, and the next day they sent us for a CT scan.

The morning after the CT was the morning of New Year's Eve. My phone rang around 9:00 a.m., and it was our pediatrician. "Mrs.

Ebo, the CT showed a mass in the adrenal gland above Audra's right kidney. We need you to get downtown to the children's hospital and go directly to the fifth floor as soon as possible. I've already called them, and they're expecting you."

Tim had walked in while I was listening to the doctor's words and could see what he was saying written all over my face. "What is it?" he asked loudly. I said, "Don't leave this room," and finished the conversation with the doctor. After I hung up, I sat down, conveyed the message and tried to work through the shock. I remember it taking forever to get ready and get to the hospital. It was less than thirty miles away, but I felt like my whole world was moving in slow motion.

Meeting Dr. Ron was such a God-send. First, he showed Tim and me the CT pictures. The primary tumor had taken over a large part of her right side. There was no lump because the tumor spread out like octopus tentacles and wrapped around everything inside her body instead of pushing out. Then, he explained that further tests were needed, but he was pretty sure Audra had Neuroblastoma, a solid tumor cancer. My sweet husband responded through tears, "I'm going to need you to help me out here. My father passed away from cancer, so all I can see is a bad ending." Dr. Ron reassured us that he understood and could not have done this job for thirty years if he didn't truly believe that every child that came through the hospital doors had the potential to be cured. His exact response was, "Why not Audra?" He refused to deal in odds because he was not God. I'm not sure if that is what brought up our faith in Christ, but somehow it came up in conversation. Dr. Ron expressed his faith in Jesus, and God gave us peace that our daughter was in good hands.

We returned to Audra's room to explain to her what we had learned. We were visibly shaken, and it frightened her. We told her that the scan showed a tumor, and she had cancer. She replied, "Zoe, (her oldest sister) says that people die from cancer." Tim answered, "Some do, but we're going to do everything we can to keep that from happening to you. Ultimately God has the final say. We're going to trust Him."

Audra was admitted to the hospital that night. We got settled into our beds, and I saw fireworks in the distance from our window. I said, "Look, Audra! Someone is setting off fireworks. I forgot it's New Year's Eve!" Then I heard her softly cry. I said, "Do you want to talk about it?" She quietly and desperately responded, "I'm just afraid I'll never have a dog." I held her until she fell asleep. Then I called her dad and relayed her concerns. He said, "Oh, she'll have a dog!" We were powerless to fix her cancer problem, but we could definitely get her a dog.

Over the next thirteen days, Neuroblastoma was confirmed. Tests showed she had sixteen places of disease, three spots on her lungs, and her bone marrow was full of cancer. They placed a central line for her and started me on the education fast track for her care. Our lives were spiraling away from everything that looked familiar. During a training session with the nurse educator, Audra cried out, "I just want to be normal!" My heart sank. She had been so strong through all of it. I held her as she cried and reassured her, "Cancer sucks! It's not fair, and it's never going to be fair. But we have someone with us that helps us. Jesus never promised us we wouldn't have trouble, in fact, He said the opposite. What He promised is that He would take all the trouble and use it for our good. We're just going to have to actively search for the good."

Most days, that's exactly what it was, a search for the good. But every day God was weaving for us a new perspective, an eternal perspective. We learned to celebrate more, seize more opportunities, and cherish the mundane. Normal days, the ones we recognized as our precancer normal, looked so beautiful when they showed up from time to time. Our schedule was typically insane. Audra spent 180 days in 2015 admitted to the hospital. On top of that were clinic visits, line care, medications, and the relentless threat of infection. The stress was overwhelming. And right along side of growing stress was equally growing grace. With every piece of challenging information we would receive, God would send an equal or greater blessing our way. We were able to buy a business, move to a new house that improved our everyday life, get a dog, spend more time with extended family, take trips of a lifetime to Disney, the Biltmore, the Atlanta Aquarium, to see and meet the Christian artist Carman, to build a playhouse Audra always wanted, get a pool, an off-roading go kart, and watch her enjoy a shopping spree, not to mention the countless packages and cards that came in the mail, and the list goes on, but only because of the grace of God and the generosity He moved through others.

One day Audra asked me, "Mom, why do people give me stuff?" How do you answer that without drawing more attention to the elephant in the room? "I think it's because suffering is something every human being understands, and most people want to relieve suffering in themselves and others. Adults especially find suffering in children to be unacceptable. I think they just want you to be as happy as you can be." She didn't have a response, but that usually meant she was thinking it over.

Audra came to complete surrender one night at church. She was only twelve and found her way to declare, "Lord, if You want to call me home, then let the scan results show the cancer is back. But if You have a purpose for me, then let the scans be clear. Whatever You want is OK with me." Only God can impart faith to a child that resembles the faith of the apostle Paul, "For to me, to live is Christ and to die is gain. If I am to go on living in the body, this will mean fruitful labor for me. Yet what shall I choose? I do not know! I am torn between the two: I desire to depart and be with Christ, which is better by far; but it is more necessary for you that I remain in the body" (Philippians 1:21-24 NIV). She received a lasting peace that night as a result of her faith in God. It carried her through until the end.

Why am I dedicating an entire chapter to my daughter? Through the life, suffering and eventual death of my little girl, God taught and is still teaching me more than I ever wanted to learn. We almost lost her three times during treatment. Being separated as a family could have easily destroyed our home life. But God, showed up and restored her to health for seven months of normal before the cancer came back. Those months have become precious to us as a family. For Audra, they were seven months of growing in deep affection for Jesus Christ. I have never witnessed that closely the maturing of a Christian life. She became an inspiration to me and to many others—hands raised in praise to God until the end. When she passed away, it was ugly and painful, but she was beautiful through it all. Her final few moments on earth were stressful. At the height of that stress, Jesus entered the room. She spoke to Him, and her final words were, "I believe, I believe You are good."

We have never experienced the arms of Jesus hold us as tightly as they did during Audra's fight with cancer. With every prayer offered on Audra's behalf and ours, we were surrounded by grace and underneath us were the Everlasting Arms. There are many who are reading this book that did not know our family at the time, but there are so many who did. You knew, and you prayed. You prayed the words we could not. You locked arms with others around the world and lifted us before the throne of God. And we felt it every, single, day. Thank you. I thank God because of you. And I thank God "for the gracious favor granted us in answer to the prayers of many" (2 Corinthians 1:8-11).

Chapter Nine

Able, Willing, Sovereign

When we received Audra's official diagnosis of cancer, my husband called the kids and our mothers together to give them the news. Tim further explained that the next couple of years would be difficult, and that it would require a great deal of patience and understanding. The kids asked questions like, "Is she coming home? Is she scared? Is she going to die?" He talked through each question and provided answers when there were answers. Then Tim told them there was one question we would not ask: we would never ask God, "Why?" He told them that it was a pointless question because we could never, with our finite minds, comprehend the workings of the Infinite God. He reiterated that we trust God. Our trust in Him is not dependent on our circumstances.

Tim reminded them of the story of Shadrach, Meshach, and Abednego. Specifically, he recounted their stance before the king in Daniel chapter three (ESV). As the story goes, King Nebuchadnezzar made an image of himself out of pure gold that stood ninety feet tall. When the music played, the entire kingdom was required to bow down and worship the idol. The three Hebrews stood alone in the crowd, refusing to worship anyone but the One true God. Nebuchadnezzar was livid. The consequence for their disobedience was to be thrown into a furnace of blazing fire. The king taunted them saying, "And who is the god who will deliver you out of my hands?" (v. 15). Shadrach, Meshach, and Abednego responded with confidence in their God, "O Nebuchadnezzar, we have no need to answer you in this matter. If this be so, our God whom we serve is able to deliver us from the burning fiery furnace, and he will deliver us out of your hand, O king. *But if not*, be it known to you, O king, that we will not serve your gods or worship the golden image you have set up" (v. 16-18 emphasis added).

This infuriated the king. He responded by having the furnace heated seven times hotter and gave the order for the young men to be bound. The furnace was so hot, the men who carried Shadrach, Meshach, and Abednego to the flame were killed. What Nebuchadnezzar witnessed in the furnace makes my heart leap for joy. There were not three, but four in the fire—unbound, walking around, unharmed. We drew strength from God's miraculous deliverance of Shadrach, Meshach, and Abednego. Our minds were set by the faith of those three, and their response became our mantra. We know that our God is able to heal Audra. We believe that He will. But if He does not, we will continue to trust Him because He is sovereign, and He knows what is best.

It's not easy to stand in the face of an enemy who appears to hold all the power whether it be a king or cancer. But I think our confidence is secured when we recognize our enemy's power is cut short every time by our God's authority. Our God reigns, and He reigns in absolute power. And what makes us more than conquerors? He is for us. He has taken a side, and it's ours.

God's sovereignty is so interwoven with His heart and His character that His rightful place in the universe does not negate His compassionate concern for me, His love for me, and His Presence at my right hand. He does not distribute good and evil on a whim like a Greek or Roman god made in the image of man. Cancer was never God's plan for man; it did not exist in the garden. It is a result of sin. Man's violation of man mentally, emotionally and physically was not birthed in God's heart nor is it dispensed from God's hand. In Christ we are not enemies of God, therefore He has no reason to treat us as such.

However we do have an enemy intent on destroying us and our perception of our God. 1 Peter 5:8 (ESV) says, "Be alert and of sober mind. Your enemy the devil prowls around like a roaring lion looking for someone to devour." There are times I have been deceived by the enemy and guilty of attributing to God what is not God. In my attempt to make sense of the pain and torment of Audra's swelling brain tumors, I have searched for God in the cause of her pain. I have looked for God's hand in the event of her relentless suffering, and I have failed to find Him where He is not. "God isn't in the event. He is in the response to the event and the love that is shown and the care that is given" (Call the Midwife, Season 3, Episode 4). God was not speaking through the serpent tempting Eve. He was not the motivator of Adam to eat the forbidden fruit. He was however, completely responsible for the redemption of mankind. God's sovereignty does not indict God for the wrongs of man or the effects of sin. It does, however, enable Him to take upon Himself the sole responsibility of setting all wrongs right.

God did deliver Shadrach, Meshach and Abednego from the king's hand. When Nebuchadnezzar saw them on their stroll through the furnace, he ordered them out. The Bible says, "The hair of their heads was not singed, their cloaks were not harmed, and no smell of fire had come upon them" (Daniel 3:27 ESV). Their confidence and conviction to love the Lord their God and serve Him only brought about faith in God for the king, as well, who said, "… there is no other god who is able to rescue in this way" (Daniel 3:29 ESV).

God has not changed. He is able today to accomplish more than we know how to imagine. He is willing to come to our aid in every situation. He has the final say in all things. Jesus walked through the fires of cancer with Audra. He guarded her heart with the perspective of eternity. He surrounded her with songs of deliverance. He walked her out of the furnace into the safety of heaven. Cancer can never touch her again. Audra refused to bow to the idols of fear and doubt. The number of people who have been influenced for God because she stood is still being counted. There is no other god who is able to rescue in this way.

We don't like to use the words, "If not." That means we must acknowledge that God may have a different plan than our own. That means we have to make room for His authority over us as well as His authority over our enemy. This mantra does not mean we have experienced smooth sailing through this journey. We are not all sitting around fondly remembering the last three years. It means through the heartache, frustration, tears, pain and sorrow, we stand knowing Who we serve—knowing He is for us, and He will get us through somehow.

I struggled with this chapter because I was unsure how to explain the words able, willing, and sovereign when I continue to be taught by them. I have not arrived in my discernment, and I do not think I will with my current human limitations. God's deliverance for our three Bible friends was immediate and in this life. His plan for our family was different. Does that mean that in our case, He was able and sovereign but not willing? According to *Miriam-Webster*, being willing means one is "inclined or favorably ready; prompt to act or respond." God was never a spectator of Audra's cancer. He was always there, consistently acting and responding favorably to her cries for help. I do not know the ins and outs of God's plan for us. He didn't ask me to sign off on it. I have come to understand that knowing God as able, willing, and sovereign leaves some questions unanswered. And just like I have come to accept that He is three persons in one without being able to make perfect sense of the Trinity, I have to allow that God is more than I can contain within my thoughts. It is vital that I trust in His good character to prevail.

A few days before Audra died, Tim gathered the kids one more time to let them know it would be soon. This time he spoke of how Audra's suffering was coming to an end and that we could be assured she was getting ready to experience the best of what God has promised. The most honest and faith-filled words I have ever heard him say came next, "We know this is what's best for Audra, and I have to believe that somehow, some way, God is going to work this out to be what's best for our family." The truth is, we may never see with our earthly eyes how it is best. But faith is the substance of things hoped for, the evidence of things not seen (Hebrews 11:1 NKJV). This earth is not the end. I have never been more convinced of our eternal future.

Recalling Audra's suffering is difficult. Living it with her was brutal. Knowing that God's plan extends into eternity is redeeming. I know that our circumstances in this life are not preparation merely for this life. God is not wasteful, random, moody or selfish. I believe that all Audra endured was worked by God's hand into a perfect reward that she now continually enjoys. For me, there is a hole, a void in the time and space of my daily life, but God has given me the capacity to say, "It is well with my soul." My eternal well-being is secure. I am complete, whole in Christ, no matter how I feel. Every day is a challenge and a miracle. And I am convinced that I will see with my eyes someday the good that God has brought about for the rest of us who continue to trust Him as we suffer from losing her.

The tone was set for our family as we walked out the end of Audra's life. It was set from the beginning. God had been stretching and growing our understanding so that we would have the tools necessary to weather the storm. It does not matter the swells, the tides, the violent skies that you are facing today. The circumstances you are in make no difference to God. He comes to us the same in every situation—He is Able, He is Willing, and He is Sovereign.

Chapter Ten

Order My Steps

"I want to leave!" I shouted. "Well, too bad," he responded, "You wanted to talk, and we're going to finish our talk." The whole week had been singularly charged with stress and frustration, and Tim and I ended up on a collision course. We went head on into one of the most emotionally uncontrolled fights of our relationship. This was not in the early years. It was after twenty-three years of marriage.

We screamed until it became yelling. We yelled until it became regretful crying. Then we got to the heart of the matter. Tim's mind had been circling around caring for the needs of his mom. She was sick, and there was no clear solution. My mind was focused on the needs at home, and that day being home was very difficult. I had to go through what was left of Audra's things. The sadness enveloped me. "I needed you today, and you weren't here," I explained. I continued, "I know it wasn't your fault. You needed to help your mom. I understand, but I did everything I knew to overcome your absence, and it didn't work." That's when I began to second guess everything I have learned and everything I have tried to share in this book. I wanted to quit writing because, even after going to God, I chose to demand from Tim. I chose to look to Tim for something he wasn't meant to give. Standing directly in light of truth, I still chose poorly.

Eventually, our fight turned into a discussion. The blame speech lost momentum, and the truth penetrated our defenses. We were both so angry, but not with each other. We were fighting each other because we lost sight of our real enemy. We were easy targets for one another. In the aftermath, I saw how disappointed he was. He saw how hurt I was. Thank God, we chose to stay in the same room, ride out the storm, and find our way through the turbulence of emotion back to each other.

When it was over, I felt like I had gone ten rounds with the champ. Not because I had been sparring with Tim, but because I took the bait of the enemy to think only of myself. I insisted on my rights and became unwilling to suffer for an evening, let alone suffer long. My mind was filled with only me, and I became a dissatisfied woman on a mission to salve my pain.

In an argument where I am the only thing on my mind, I say things. I do not utilize a filter. I don't think to myself, "I can never take this back, so I better not say it." I just let the insults roll right off my tongue. And this time I sat back in horror as I watched them continue to burn into the soul of the person I love most in this world. Tim and I reached resolution that night. We did not go to bed angry with each other, but we were threatened by self-loathing even into the next day. I remember repeatedly asking God to cover and heal the wounds that I inflicted on Tim. Thank God, He is faithful.

I asked the Lord, "Why does this keep happening?" I demanded an answer as to why God has not completed this work in me. He has already given me the plan and power to go to Him instead of Tim. He has healed my perspective on marriage and created a solid covenant between us. So much has changed in our relationship since it began that I could fill volumes. So why were we compelled once again to claw and grasp for our needs?

God did not speak to my heart like He has done in the past. Instead a picture started forming in my mind that over time is becoming clearer. I see me striving for perfection. I see Jesus already perfect. He is not looking at me in condemnation, wishing I would get it right once and for all. His arms are wide open to receive me and hide me in His perfection—the only perfection I can ever know on this earth.

The vision of God's way shed light on my slightly askew view of the Christian life. I spend so much time trying to give the right impression of Who God is through my excellent example that I forget the world is supposed to see Jesus, not me. It's not my job to display perfection. My job is to point to the Perfect One, especially when I prove to be imperfect. If I'm honest, I only ever doubt the validity of God's principles when I fail to live up to them. I am weighed, measured, and found wanting more often than I care to admit. And I feel like throwing in the towel because of how it makes me look and feel. That has nothing to do with God. God is God, and His ways are right whether I obey or not. We need to stop putting our reputation in the place designated for God's. God and I have a relationship that works because of God, not because of me.

Jesus died to rescue mankind from an eternal fate dictated by sin. Romans 6:23 (NIV) warns, "For the wages of sin is death; but the gift of God is eternal life in Jesus Christ our Lord." I have earned death. The condition of depravity that I have inherited from the original sin of Adam makes me destined for separation from God, not to mention the countless choices I've made in sin and selfishness. Jesus rescued me from eternal destruction, so that I might live with Him forever. He did not die merely to raise my self-image or improve my public relations. Salvation goes much deeper than how things appear.

Please don't take my description of the inexhaustible grace of God as an excuse to stay the way you are. God accepts us where we are, just as we are. But His desire is for us to be Holy. In fact, He commands it in Leviticus 11:45 (ESV), "Be holy for I am holy." It is frustrating to think we will never achieve our own perfection in this life. But does that mean we should quit trying, wallow in our imperfection, and live the way we want? By no means! It's better to shoot for the moon and miss than aim for a skunk and hit it. Or so I've been told. We have already covered the ground of obedience and its importance. God has given us the capacity to obey. We should always strive to be obedient. At the same time, be mindful that we are imperfect, and we will fail. Psalm 73:26 (ESV) says, "My flesh and my heart may fail, but God is the strength of my heart and my portion forever." Lamentations 3:22-23 (ESV) reminds us, "The steadfast love of the Lord never ceases; his mercies never come to an end; they are new every morning; great is your faithfulness."

We do have a responsibility to represent Christ well. "We are ambassadors for Christ, God making his appeal through us" (2 Corinthians 5:20 ESV). The balance is found by asking ourselves, if God is making His appeal through us, what exactly is His appeal? To live right? To behave well? To pretend we have arrived? If we back up to verse 19, we see more clearly, "... in Christ God was reconciling the world to himself, not counting their trespasses against them, and entrusting to us the message of reconciliation." We are the physical vessels in which Christ moves and breathes in this world. "We implore you on behalf of Christ, be reconciled to God. For our sake he made him to be sin who knew no sin, so that in him we might become the righteousness of God" (2 Corinthians 5:20-21 ESV). In other words, we are invited at God's urgent request to be peacemakers between God and mankind. His appeal is restored relationship. Right living happens to be the greatest by-product the world has ever known, and it comes only through right relationship with God.

"The steps of good men are directed by the Lord. He delights in each step they take. If they fall, it isn't fatal, for the Lord upholds them with his hand" (Psalm 37:23-24 TLB). His desire is to walk with me and bridge the gap when I miss the mark. That way, when I mess up His perfection becomes visible like bright light against the darkness. When I am weak, if I stay linked with Him, He is revealed. He shows His love for me and provides solutions and healing. He hears my confession and makes good on His promises with forgiveness and revelation. He restores my dignity with His Presence and reminds me that these failures are becoming fewer and farther in between. And just as quickly as the Spirit lifts away, He freely returns to rest on me in the peace of God once again.

I want God to be pleased with me. I believe He is most pleased with me when I am most dependent on Him. He doesn't want me to screw up my life. But God does not want me to try to fix it on my own either—that's not trust. That's not possible. Adam and Eve tried to cover their own sin with leaves. It was a temporary, feeble fix for an eternal problem. God knew exactly what to do. He moved in with sacrificial love and made an enduring wardrobe, a durable covering for His children that would withstand the wear and tear of an imperfect nature. They were wrong, but He was always right and had the plan and power to make them right again and keep them right.

Have you ever had a day that spiraled downward so fast your number one desire was to put it in the past and wake the next day to His new mercies? If you have, you have plenty of company. Don't give up when you fail. It is the best time to inquire of the Lord. 1 John 1:9 (NKJV) instructs us, "If we confess our sins, He is faithful and just to forgive us our sins and to cleanse us from all unrighteousness." Agree with God that you failed. Seek first forgiveness, cleansing, and then understanding. Learn from your mistakes. Press on toward the goal of holy living while pressing in to the One Who is already holy.

Oh, and one more thing. After you have let God set you right with Him, remember to set things right with anyone else who may be affected by your failure. Asking Tim for forgiveness is not as hard as it was in the beginning. I have more confidence in our love for each other now than I did when we were first married. Relaying to our kids how it is wrong for us to handle ourselves in anger, is a little more difficult. I hate failing Tim, but he is an adult and understands the pressures. Children tend to worry and feel insecure. The first step, at least with my kids, is to make no excuses and approach each one in humility. Then restore their security by explaining that our disagreements do not mean an end to our family as we know it.

People fight. Each one of us is a unique creation, and our differences can cause conflict. But even fights can be redeemed by God to work for our good. We don't freely sin, rebel, or disobey just because we know that God can compensate for our poor behavior. But when we do find ourselves fallible, we rejoice that God can and does generously redeem. Therefore, I write with sanctified resolve, His ways are true. I am not the proof. He is.

Chapter Eleven

God is Good

I was driving slowly and cautiously, trying to see through the tears. I could hear the doctor's words on a continuous loop in my mind, "You are pregnant, but there is no sign of life. It's just a matter of time before your body will take over and finish the process." She was kind but matter of fact. I remember searching her face for any hope. And I remember the Holy Spirit, at the same time, moving on my heart with reminders of eternal hope. The mental loop was interrupted by my phone. It was Tim. He couldn't wait for me to get home. He wanted to know why I was pregnant and bleeding. "What's the official word?" he said. "It's only a matter of time now according to the doctor," I responded wearily. In an effort to stand strong he said, "What's your confession?" I believe our confession, our verbal admission of the truth of God, is so important. But I have come to understand, it is not our confession that is all powerful. Our confession is simply our response to an all-powerful God. I had no confidence that I knew what to claim, and then an answer rose up from my spirit, "God is good. I trust the Lord."

I'm pretty sure that is not what he was looking for. He was looking for me to stand with him in faith that this child would survive, that we would get what we wanted. He wasn't ignorant of the Word or manipulative in any way. He was hurting and trying to ease the pain in me. I could not form solid faith ground on my own. I had been down this road too many times to really believe that I knew what was best for me. I always know what I want. I just don't always have a clear grasp on what God wants for me. The Lord replied through me, and His confession changed my perspective. God is good. I trust the Lord.

What is good? What does it mean? I looked up the definition online and found at least twenty-five different ways we use the word good. So do we really know what good is? Psalm 119:68 states,

"You are good, and what you do is good" (NIV). From Genesis to Revelation we are given snapshots of the goodness of God. Jesus, Himself, declared "No one is good except God alone" (Mark 10:18 NIV). The Psalms sing of His goodness, "The Lord is good to all; he has compassion on all he has made" (145:9 NIV).

Nahum 1:7 (NIV) encourages us, "The Lord is good, a refuge in times of trouble. He cares for those who trust in him …" How does that play out when we find ourselves in harm's way? I have spent my life learning to trust in Him. There are many others I know who trust in Him, and yet we all suffer right along with those who do not trust in Him. Matthew 5:45 (NIV) reveals, "He causes His sun to rise on the evil and the good, and sends rain on the righteous and unrighteous." Does that describe God as our refuge? Is He actively caring for us? Psalm 84:11 (ESV) assures us, "No good thing does He withhold from those who walk uprightly." Isn't food a good thing? There are people starving in the world. Some of those people are Christians. Are they starving because God is withholding food? Or maybe, God forbid, we think we can discern from this verse that those starving must not be walking uprightly?

Every question leads to more questions, and I cannot fully satisfy any of them. I have not been given any secrets. All I want to do is pose one more line of questioning, one of perspective. Can God be good and do good in a world where mankind suffers? Does the fact that we suffer negate God's goodness? And can suffering, when cast in an eternal light, produce a greater good than a life with no suffering? If we only see good from our perspective, what good are we giving up?

Genesis 3:6 (ESV) recounts, "So when the woman saw that the tree was good for food, and that it was a delight to the eyes, and that the tree was to be desired to make one wise, she took of its fruit and ate, and she also gave some to her husband who was with her, and he ate." From Eve's perspective the food was good, delightful looking, and eating it would yield a desired result. The actual result was the onset of the very suffering with which we struggle. Was her choice God's fault? He told her the truth and instructed her stay away from it. She trusted her own instincts instead of God's Word. Adam trusted Eve.

When God created man and woman, He called His creation good. However, I have heard the question more than once, "Why would God create man knowing man would have to suffer?" As if suffering on man's part negates the good in God creating him. In my estimation, RT Kendall asked the better question, the one no one asks, "Why would God create man, knowing God Himself would have to suffer?" How quickly we forget, that "He was pierced for our transgressions, He was crushed for our iniquities; the punishment that brought us peace was on him, and by his wounds we are healed" (Isaiah 53:5 NIV). I am not trying to dismiss the difficult questions of man's existence. I am merely trying to consider that there is another perspective—a perfect one, I might add.

The story of Joseph, found in Genesis, is an example that shifts perspective. He was the little brother of ten older brothers. They were supposed to protect and instruct him. Joseph was their father's favorite, so they hated him. They hated him enough to sell him into slavery and tell their father that Joseph was dead. Even after the hardship of being repeatedly wronged, Joseph chose to see things from God's perspective. He was raised by the power of God from slave to Pharaoh's right-hand man. God gave him specific wisdom to make provision for all of Egypt to survive a coming famine. The Bible says the famine was so severe everywhere that all the world came to Egypt to buy grain, including Joseph's brothers. Joseph was able to save his entire family through the plan and power of God.

He was reunited with his father, who lived seventeen more years in Egypt before he died. Upon their father's death, his brothers feared Joseph would finally exact his revenge. Instead, Joseph trusted in God. "Do not be afraid, for am I in the place of God? [Vengeance is His, not mine.] As for you, you meant evil against me, but God meant it for good in order to bring about this present outcome, that many people would be kept alive [as they are this day] (Genesis 50:19-20 AMP). I am certain that Joseph had to work through anger as his life moved from one set of unfair circumstances to another. But in the end, would he have chosen to change his story? Would he have been willing to forfeit his family's survival for his own temporary comfort? Knowing the real outcome now, what would Eve give to have drawn a different conclusion before she ate the forbidden fruit? Would Adam, if given another chance, lovingly refuse his wife?

When we choose for ourselves what is good and what is the desirable outcome of our circumstances, are we actually settling for less? We are limited in our vision. We cannot see the end from the beginning. In my own life, my perspective has often left me frustrated. All I saw was a marriage about to fail, desperate need for rest, peace, and emotional stability, and the agony of great loss on every level. Good? It didn't look good to me at the time. But trusting in God has helped me to see His ways bring about a much greater good than my immediate satisfaction.

None of what I am relaying to you is natural or easy or even something we can accomplish on our own. Also, we cannot go back, but we can move forward. This all boils down to trusting God, trusting His goodness enough to follow Him through the messy darkness, one step at a time. And staying on the path with Him until we are standing in the light of His plan for our lives. His plan works all things to benefit us, and miraculously, it benefits those around us as well. I think of my husband and children. Every choice I made to align myself with God became a blessing for my family, too. I cannot even imagine where we would have been following my plan for our lives.

What does it mean to follow His plan? What does it mean to stay on the path? I think the key is to surrender our expectation and allow God to open our eyes with His expectation. In other words, stop looking for immediate results that reflect what we define as good. I can't tell you how many times, even while writing this book, that my declarations of faith have been challenged. I have been tempted to question, "How can I say this book is true when my behavior, my performance is still greatly lacking?" This question arises only when my little world undergoes a shaking. It rises to the surface right along with my temper, impatience, negative emotions, and selfishness. But it's only because those things can be shaken. After the dust settles, I consistently find myself clinging to the unshaken faith in Christ that remains. In this way He continues to escort me further up and further in to His Kingdom.

Would I have chosen to know personally the four babies I lost? Yes. Would I have chosen to remove Audra's suffering and have her here with me today? Of course. Do I wish we would have been totally independent instead of living with family members for thirteen years of our marriage? Do I regret that because of our former living situation, we are often still misunderstood? Yes, and yes again. Do I beg God to heal the wounds I have caused in my husband and children with careless words spoken in anger? Absolutely. But God is with me, encouraging me through every frustration and difficulty and even through every failure. He reminds me that it's not over! That does not always change the way I feel, but it does change the way I respond. Only a good God would walk with His children through this life, giving help when help is needed. And His goodness is so far reaching, it does not end in this life. It reaches all the way throughout eternity.

I quoted Psalm 119:68 earlier. I would like to shed light on the verse prior to it, *"Before I was afflicted* I went astray, But now I keep and honor Your word [with loving obedience]. You are good and do good; Teach me Your statutes" (Psalm 119:67-68 AMP accent mine). For the Psalmist, affliction, which never seems good, was worked for him like an anchor. Affliction held him fast to the ways of God, and proved God's goodness in his life. Am I now praying that affliction will find me? Not exactly, but I pray that I will never move far from God, and always pursue a life with Him no matter what finds me. I trust that with each season of inquiring, I am growing closer to my Lord. If no other good comes out of my life but the increasing ability to keep and honor God's Word with loving obedience, it would be more good than I could imagine—good that keeps on getting better and never ends—even if it is worked out in response to affliction.

God's goodness is not dependent upon what happens to me. I do not interpret what is good by how I feel or what I see. I trust that God's Word gives me growing insight into Who He is, and by that standard I confess, God is good, I trust the Lord!

A Grief Conserved

"Dear Jesus, Audra is gone. Writing that hurts so much. It is beyond comforting that I know she is with You. She is being rewarded, she is at peace with her flesh, she is complete in You. She is more than happy—FOREVER! I don't even know how to fully grasp that. I'm just so glad she is NEVER alone. Thank You for carrying her through these last two years. Now please ... carry me ... because, right now, I am none of those things."

That was my journal entry after losing my daughter. I entitled this portion of the book, "A Grief Conserved" because as I write this, I've been maintaining my grief fairly well. My habit has become to only go near my grief briefly and try not to touch or arouse it. The problem is, the less I acknowledge it, the more it screams for my attention. The more I try to leave it behind me, the more I see it waiting ahead for me.

Gaining some form of emotional stability in my life was a difficult process. I discovered how to keep from indulging emotional urges and the way to identify which negative emotions I should deny in order to keep my actions an asset to God's kingdom. The problem with grief is that those methods don't work, and are actually detrimental to healing.

Audra passed almost eight months ago, and I think the swell of grief has grown into a full-blown tsunami. We just finished Thanksgiving and are doing our best to stare down Christmas. Strife has reared its ugly head daily in our home as my younger ones deal the only way they know how. My girls have gravitated toward each other, painfully trying to fill the gap. Tim and I are stepping on each other's toes a little more often lately. According to all I have read and listened to by the experts, we're right on track. That's both reassuring and disturbing.

I am moving forward with C.S. Lewis's, *A Grief Observed*. I can empathize with much of what he expresses, "The act of living is different all through. Her absence is like the sky, spread over everything." Strangely, I find the most helpful piece of advice comes from his statement, "Aren't all these notes the senseless writings of a man who won't accept the fact that there is nothing we can do with suffering except to suffer it?"

I don't know that grief can be fully understood. It cannot be explained away. It can't be avoided, contained, ignored, transferred, hurried along, defeated, or mastered. It can, however, be shared, shouldered like a burden, by those who love you and most importantly by the God Who blesses us with the promised comfort when we mourn. I thought I knew what to expect from comfort. I now know that God's comfort looks very different from what I envisioned. I find comfort only in the presence of Jesus, and like manna from heaven, it must be collected every day.

If you have suffered great loss. Please reach out, reach up. We were not meant to live out the good days of this life like an island. We were created to be together, sharing one another's lives, the joys and the sorrows. There is only one way through grief, to suffer it. But it need not be suffered in silence or alone.

Works Cited

Hemfelt, Dr. Robert and Fowler, Dr. Richard. *Serenity, A Companion for Twelve Step Recovery*, Thomas Nelson, 1990, pp. 15-16.

Miriam-Webster Online, s.v. "serenity," accessed November 2017, www.miriam-webster.com.

Omartian, Stormie. *The Power of a Praying Parent*, Harvest House Publishing 1995, pp. 29.

Call the Midwife. "Season 3, Episode 4," Directed by Juliet May. Written by Jennifer Worth, Heidi Thomas, Gabbie Asher. BBC February 9, 2014.

Miriam-Webster Online, s.v. "willing," accessed November 2017, www.miriam-webster.com.

Lewis, C.S. *A Grief Observed*, HarperCollins e-books May 2009, pp. 24, 44-45.

About the Author

Melanie Ebo is a follower of Christ and has been since childhood. Nothing has marked her life more than spiritual formation. She lives in a small town outside of Columbia, SC with her husband and seven children. Melanie has served the Lord for the last twenty-five years as pastor's wife, worship  leader, speaker, small group leader, mom, homeschooler, and friend. Now she is officially a writer. Her love for the Word of God and pursuit of all things Jesus have not perfected her, yet. But she is relying on the promise of God that "He has made everything beautiful in his time. Also, he has put eternity into man's heart ..." (Ecclesiastes 3:11, ESV). Looking forward to heaven and all who wait for her there, Melanie remains committed to knowing God and His purpose for her here.